101 Activities for English Language Learning

Content-based Ideas with Easy Re-sources

Charles F. Hirsch
and Deborah Lazarus
Illustrated by Yoshi Miyake

Rigby Best Teachers Press
An imprint of Rigby • A division of Reed Elsevier, Inc.

For more information about other books from Rigby Best Teachers Press, please contact
Rigby at 800-822-8661 or **www.rigby.com**

Editor: Georgine Cooper, and Pam Gunter
Executive Editor: Laura Strom
Designer: Biner Design
Design Project Manager: Tom Sjoerdsma
Cover photograph: Sharon Hoogstraten
Interior Illustrator: Yoshi Miyake

06 05 04 03 02
10 9 8 7 6 5 4 3 2

Printed in the United States of America.

ISBN 0-7635-7346-9
101 Activities for English Language Learning

CONTENTS

Imagine that you have a resource as large as the Library of Congress—books, pictures, music, maps, periodicals. Add to that the contents of a teaching supply superstore—free reproducibles, clip art, stickers, craft projects. What's more, it is portable. You can carry it with you all over the world, and from it you reach most corners of the world. Trouble is, it's all been dumped on the floor, and you have to sort through it. That was our, the authors', early experience with the Internet as we began to discover what it could do for us as ELL teachers. Our mission was to find out how we harness its range and power for ELL programs and to create a resource for our colleagues who would like to do the same.

101 Activities for English Language Learning is designed to provide content-based language learning activities for children in grades one through four with a special focus on mining the rich resources of the Internet. It is for teachers—both new and experienced—who are ready to add a new dimension to their teaching by exploring the possibilities available in cyberspace. Our goal is to help you incorporate new teaching strategies, as well as to enrich what you already do in the classroom.

> *101 Activities for English Language Learning* is designed to provide content-based language learning activities for children in grades one through four with a special focus on mining the rich resources of the Internet.

One hundred of these activities are for use with your children. The activity contained at the end of this introduction is created just for you. This teacher activity serves two purposes: to put you in touch with your unique and powerful talents and to provide a preview of and practice for the activities you will be doing with the children.

101 Activities offers you the flexibility to choose from a collection of activities that work in a variety of learning environments. Are you teaching small pull-out classes of English-language learners? Are you a grade-level teacher looking for activities that include English-language learners within the whole group of learners? You may be a bilingual teacher who can use these activities to supplement English-only instruction. You may even be a resource room teacher working with special needs students, and you will select some of these teaching strategies for small group work. Most of these activities may be easily adapted for your children and your particular setting.

The Internet references—called R*e*-sources—support the activities in a variety of ways. Some provide background or reference material for the teacher. Others contain resources that can be printed out or downloaded for use with students. Still others can be viewed or used interactively.

101 Activities engages English-language learners first in speaking and listening, then in reading and writing. The activities, reproducibles, literature selections, and songs provide opportunities for newcomers to English to master language through content at a variety of levels.

Since English-language learners must learn language and content simultaneously, each activity is connected to one or more content area. Because fluency level can vary widely in a single group of learners, the activities encompass a variety levels.

Some students may be at the level of non-verbal response. Others have basic vocabulary. Still others are ready to use more elaborate sentence structure and language patterns. We have, therefore, labeled the activities by suggested levels (See the "How to Use This Book" section of the introduction, page 6). Many of the beginning level activities are appropriate for all levels. Some of the intermediate and advanced activities can be adapted for use with a wider range of learners in cooperative learning groups. As you preview the activities, keep in mind that you know your students better than we do; feel free to adapt and enhance the activities to suit your needs and the needs of your students.

To keep students involved, *101 Activities* presents techniques and strategies that engage multiple learning styles. When students work together using technology, begin to interact, organize and plan tasks, and ask questions, their learning is enhanced. The Internet engages a student's hands, eyes, ears, and mind to foster language learning.

How to Use this Book

101 Activities can be used for supplementing, supporting, and enhancing existing current curriculum. In the absence of a formal or detailed curriculum, the activities can be used as a launching point for building your curriculum. Pick and choose. Adapt and modify. Make these activities your own. An address book page has been provided (page 144) for you to record your favorite sites.

The Organization

The activities are organized into twelve thematic units that support content area learning.

I Like Me	**From 1 to 100**	**Earth and Space**
We've Got the Whole World	**Weather and Seasons**	**Growing Things**
Working Together	**Big, Little, Light, Heavy**	**Critters and Creatures**
From City to Country	**Yesterday and Today**	**Celebrations**

Activities are self-contained, although they are presented in thematic units. They can be done in any order or combined within a theme to expand on or reinforce a lesson.

Activities support one or more of the following content areas:

language arts   **geography**   **history**   **fine arts**   **health**
social studies   **science**   **math**   **technology**   **physical education**

Format

The following icons are used to denote the various facets of the activities.

Key Words

The **Key Words** icon signals high utility words either taught or used in context. Most words are content area words. They are from both academic and everyday language and are reinforced as children hear, speak, and use them in an activity. Some are contained on reproducibles; others may be displayed on the board or in another appropriate format.

Subjects

The **Subjects** icon signals the related content areas.

Get Ready

The **Get Ready** icon signals the materials and resources to be gathered and any other preparation for the activities. Make sure that required materials are available, reproducibles and transparencies are prepared in advance, and Internet resources have been previewed.

The **Literature** icon signals a book or a poem to be shared with the children as part of the activity.

B I A

The **B, I,** and **A** icons signal the levels for activities: beginning, intermediate, or advanced. These are suggestions; you are the best judge of what is appropriate for your students.

Re-source

The **Re-source** icon signals one or more Internet sites that will be helpful for prior reference or for use in the activity.

How to Implement the Literature

A number of activities feature recommended fiction or nonfiction books closely tied to each unit theme. Most of them are award-winning books; some are core literature selections. Bibliographic information is provided for each of the literature selections. All books are in print and available at libraries, bookstores, or for purchase on-line.

The language for each selection is simple, predictable, and repetitive. Each piece of literature provides an authentic language pattern that students can identify, master, and then practice in everyday situations. Furthermore, in each book there is a close one-to-one relationship between text and pictures. The illustrations help put the language in context and provide clues for understanding.

The recommended books are meant to be read aloud first *by* the teacher and then by the children *with* the teacher, using shared reading techniques. Work in small groups. Preview the illustrations. Model how to track the text and choose stopping points to check for comprehension by asking questions or having students act out the meaning. After repeated re-readings, encourage students to read the book independently, with partners, or in groups. The reading can also be audiotaped so that children can listen to it in the language center. The activity for each book provides the opportunity for creative response to the literature and additional language practice.

The Internet and Re-sourcing

101 Activities lists Web sites that provide background and materials for the activities, and other recommended sites for use in small group settings. All of these sites have been previewed to ensure that the content and the links are appropriate for educational purposes and contain no offensive materials. However, Rigby is not responsible for the content of any Web site listed in this book, except their own. All material on other sites is the responsibility of the hosts and creators.

You will also need to preview the sites prior to the activity for two reasons. First, an activity may reference a site for information or to download and print out the materials. Secondly, some activities suggest viewing specific Web sites with students, and you will want to preview and bookmark these.

Consult your district's Internet policy. It likely states that children should always be supervised during Internet activities—a careful and wise practice.

Here follow some practical tips for using the Internet effectively.

Preview and Prepare

The Internet is a dynamic tool, always in motion. While it is imperfect, it is also invaluable. Advance preparation is a key to effective use. Preview the Internet sites listed in Re-sources and bookmark them (save as a favorite place). Follow the suggestions in "Get Ready" to search for and download materials. If the activity is set up for the students to use, check the commands yourself before the students begin their tasks.

During the actual lesson, call up the bookmarked site, then model and monitor the work. This presents an essential component in all of these activities: *to involve students in language learning as you invite discussion, ask questions, and engage them in hands-on work.*

• **Web site won't load:** What happens when a Web site just won't load? For example, you get the message "The page cannot be found" or "HTTP 404 - File not found." Periodic error messages occur for a number of reasons. Sometimes the page is under construction or revision. Sometimes sites are eliminated. Sometimes the address was incorrectly entered. Try the Search Skills listed on the next page. You will refine your skills the more you use the Internet.

• **Internet connections.** Connecting to your Internet Service Provider (ISP) can sometimes be slow or seem hit and miss. Check with others who use the same service to see if they have similar problems. You may also be experiencing connection problems with your modem settings or browser, such as the AOL browser, Netscape, or Internet Explorer. Contact your Internet Service Provider first. Explain the problem. Your provider may be able to offer help to modify your modem or configure your browser. Also look at your browser's Web site for search tips.

• **Slow downloading.** You may be experiencing heavy traffic, usually after school hours when everyone else is accessing the Internet. Try again at another time.

• **Access denied.** Certain filters are set up to keep hackers out, but they can keep you out as well. This is particularly true of government, university, research, and museum sites. If you are working at an institutional site, you also may have filters that can limit access. Check with your system administrator or try to access the site from your home computer. If you need the site for an activity, follow the Search Skills suggestions below for shortening a file name to access the site in a area where you can search for the particular page you want.

Search Skills

If you have been using the Internet for some time, you have probably done much of the suggested troubleshooting, but still you find that the site cannot be found. Frequently, the problem is that the page you are looking for might have been removed, had its name changed, or is temporarily, even momentarily, unavailable.

Learning to navigate the Internet requires hands-on practice. Strategies and techniques for finding the new page or replacing one that is listed are learned by doing. The following skills can help you look for what you need.

Skill 1. Try again. Hit the Refresh or Reload button and try again. Sometimes you are experiencing a momentary problem.

Skill 2. Check spelling. Internet addresses can be long and detailed. Check your use of capital or lower-case. Check to see that letters and numbers are not transposed. Check to see if hyphens, underscores, and periods are properly placed.

Skill 3. Go to the new address. Most of the time the old page returns with a message that will link you to the new Internet address. Go to that address. Preview it and bookmark the new pages that will help you with the activity.

Skill 4. Try other search engines. Some sites may have moved to other search engines or directories, such as AltaVista or Excite. Yahooligans is a secured site appropriate for children, and it is easy to find teachable materials. Talk to friends about their favorite search engines. Explore others. Over time one becomes comfortable with two or three search engines.

Skill 5. Shorten the address. Start at the end. Delete the letters or numbers following and including the last backslash (/). Work backwards. Delete each group of letters or numbers after the last slash, until you get to /main or/mainpage. You can also use this same strategy at the beginning of the address.

Follow the main page directory or index to get to the material you need. Often the site's main page will provide you with new information that you might also incorporate in these activities.

Skill 6. Add or subtract www. (include the period with www) If the address does not begin with www., add it to the beginning. If it does begin with www., then delete the letters. Proceed as in Skill 5, but start at the beginning of the address.

In addition to the array of Internet resources you will have at your fingertips, we suggest that you collect a variety of newspapers, magazines, brochures, photos, and realia (real-life objects or products) to create a stimulating environment and to use with a number of activities. Enlist the help of your students in preparing these activities. It is another way to engage students in conversation.

Finally, this book is the result of many adventures in cyberspace. We look forward to hearing about yours. Do you need help tailoring an activity to your classroom or student population? Did these activities prompt other opportunities for learning? Do you need suggestions for integrating the activities with other themes and topics? Have you created or adapted an activity based on your experience and your Internet travels? Please feel free to contact us for help or with suggestions.

cfhirsch@yahoo.com

deblazarus@yahoo.com

Just For You

Key Words

Me

Subjects

living

Get Ready

• A quiet place, your favorite music, and some private time

• Identify three gifts that you bring to your teaching. You may be nurturing in your teaching. You may be well organized or creative. Do you communicate well with parents? Do your community service activities enrich your teaching? Perhaps you draw on a special musical or artistic talent to enhance your lessons. Take some time to reflect on your talents. Then record your thoughts so you can revisit them.

• Assemble from a variety of sources a collection of pictures that reflect, describe, or otherwise represent the qualities of the gifts you have identified. Sort through the collection of pictures that you resource for your lessons. Take time to peruse some of those newspapers or magazines that have been piling up at home or at school. Using the pictures you selected, make a collage that will be a constant reminder to you of the best that you can be. For at least a week, hang the collage someplace where you'll see it often. Then place it in a desk drawer, file cabinet, or in your lesson plan book. When you find it again, it may both surprise and inspire you. Each time you revisit your collage, take a few moments to think about the gifts you continually bring to your teaching.

• Take an inexpensive, but nourishing vacation. Pamper yourself. Use the work-sheet at the right for one week. Each day do something kind, healthy, or just plain good for you—something entirely unrelated to your home or teaching responsibilities. Do it just for yourself and make it into an affirmation. (You may recognize that one or two of these affirmations pop up in things that you'll be doing with the kids later in this book.) If you can't go away for the week, plan a series of day trips to local sites you have always wanted to visit, but have never had the time.

• Once you have embarked on your Internet adventures, let us know how you're doing. Share your trials and your triumphs. Let us know what works well—what works even better than that. Re-source us at

Re-source

cfhirsch@yahoo.com for Charles Hirsch
deblazarus@yahoo.com for Debbie Lazarus

Visit **www.rigby.com** for other excellent educational resources.

Monday

Because I am special, I did this just for me.

_____

_____

Tuesday

I was especially happy today when I . . .

_____

_____

Wednesday

Today I felt really good about myself when I . . .

_____

_____

Thursday

Something I did today that I haven't done before is . . .

_____

_____

Friday

Was I ever clever today! Here's how . . .

_____

_____

Saturday

Today it really felt good to . . .

_____

_____

Sunday

You're great! Why not tell yourself how?

_____

_____

Key Words

Subjects

Get Ready

All About Me

I, like, me, he, she, him, her, his, your, my

language arts, health

I Like Me by Nancy Carlson, Puffin, 1993.
- Pocket mirrors
- Drawing paper, markers, crayons
- Chalkboard or dry-erase board
- Reproducible 1, one for each child
- Preview the Internet site below for background.

B

- Preview the cover and pictures. Encourage children to predict what the story is about. Then read the story aloud.

- After reading the story, ask children to think about things they like about themselves. Put these sentence frames on the board as prompts:

  I like my _____.   I like to _____.

- Gather children in a circle, and have them take turns completing the sentence frames. Include yourself. Follow up with "who" questions such as, *Who likes their eyes? Who likes to draw?* Have children respond using the correct names of their classmates.

- Pass out pocket mirrors to each child. Revisit the story and point out where the little pig says, "Hi, good-looking!" Encourage each child to look in the mirror and say the same thing in his or her own way.

- Have children look into the mirrors and draw a self portrait on the reproducible. Encourage them to complete the sentence frames under their pictures. Display pictures around the room and have children add more information about themselves at later dates.

Re-source

http://curry.edschool.virginia.edu/go/multicultural/activityarch.html
This page includes activities for exploring and celebrating cultural diversity. The home page provides a rich array of resources including a teacher's corner.

www.selfesteem.org
A reference for connecting with national organizations promoting self-esteem.

I like my _____.

I like to _____.

My Body

Key Words

lift, raise, stretch, point, shake, wave, hand, arm, foot, leg, head, eyes, ears, nose

Subjects

language arts, physical education

Get Ready

- Prepare a set of word cards for each child (Reproducible 2).
- Preview and bookmark the Internet site below.

B

- Review the body parts. Point to each body part and ask questions, for example, *What's this? What am I pointing to? What am I lifting?*

- As you recite the poem below, demonstrate the motions. Encourage the children to join you.

Keep on Movin'

<u>Lift</u> your <u>hand</u> up.	[Raise/Stretch–name body part]
Now put it/them down.	
Wiggle and jiggle.	
And <u>move</u> it all around.	[raise/point/shake/wave]
<u>Touch</u> your <u>head</u>.	[Point to/Shake–name body part]
<u>Wave</u> to <u>a friend</u>.	[Point to–name of child]
Wiggle and jiggle.	
Let's do it again.	

- Display a word card and demonstrate each movement. Repeat the chant. Substitute the underlined words. Make a game of it. Have volunteers lead the chant. Let the children choose a word card and correctly include it in the chant.

- Connect to **http://www.judyanddavid.com**. Click on Online Songbook. Select /H/ for <u>Hokey Pokey</u> dance. Call out actions as they dance and move to the motions.

Re-source

http://www.judyanddavid.com
A site with animation and sound.

lift	arm
raise	foot
stretch	leg
point	head
shake	eyes
wave	ears
hand	nose

My Heart

Key Words

heart, blood, heartbeat, pulse, pump, cardinal numbers 1-30

Subjects

science, math

Get Ready

- Reproducible 3, one for each child
- 3 or 4 tennis balls
- Stopwatch or large clock with second hand
- *Check that children have no activity restrictions or special health concerns.*
- Preview and bookmark the Internet site below.

- To demonstrate the heart at work, go to **http://www.innerbody.com**. Select Human Anatomy Online. Go to animations. Select Heart. You may wish to print this out.

- Have the children make a fist, hold it up, and explain that this is about the size of their heart. Tell children to show you where their own hearts are by placing their fist over their hearts. Pass out the tennis balls. Have the children take turns squeezing them as they count to ten. Make the point that the tennis balls are like the heart at work pumping blood.

- Show children how to take their own pulses. Do a ten-second pulse rate and have them record their rate on the My Heart at Rest section of the reproducible. Have children do vigorous exercise for thirty seconds (jumping jacks, run in place). Repeat ten-second pulse rates and record on My Heart at Play.

- Make two bar graphs: "The Heart at Rest" and "The Heart at Play." Use the graphs as a discussion starter to talk about how the heart works when we work, play, and rest.

Re-source

http://www.innerbody.com

http://www.yahooligans.com/science_and_nature/living_things/anatomy
Provides additional, child-friendly resources on the human body systems.

Name:

_____

My heart at rest:

_____

Name:

_____

My heart at play:

_____

My Senses

Key Words

see, hear, taste, touch, smell

Subjects

science, language arts

Get Ready

- Collect objects found in the natural world that children can see, touch, taste, smell, and hear—for example a pinecone, seashell, flowers, branches with leaves, ice, fruits and vegetables.
- Old magazines, markers, crayons
- Overhead projector
- The Five Senses (Reproducible 4)

B

- Work with the children to name the things they see displayed. Pass them around and encourage them to use their senses to get to know and talk about the objects. Use TPR (Total Physical Response) commands: *Smell the flowers. Listen to the leaves rustle. Hold the seashell up to your ear.* Make sure children practice using the verbs in different forms. Encourage them to use their imaginations. Go to **http://faculty.washington.edu/chudler/neurok.html** Check out <u>Neuroscience for Kids</u> for graphics, experiments, and games that provide further opportunities to put the senses in context.

I

- Use an overhead of Reproducible 4, The Five Senses. Select any of the objects displayed. Write the name in the first column. Then going sense by sense have the children talk about their experiences—what they see, hear, taste, touch, and smell. List their responses in the correct column. Create one poem together. It might look like this:

I see snow	I hear the snow
It feels hard.	It feels cold.
It tastes wet.	It tastes like water.
It smells cold.	It smells good.

I

- Have the children select one item to write about. Pair them with partners or divide them into small groups. Give each group a copy of the reproducible. Work with them to talk about everything they experience and sort the information into columns. Have each child write his/her own poem as you've modeled. Go to **http://faculty.washington.edu/chudler/neurok.html.** Select <u>Experiments and Activities</u>, then <u>Brain Worksheets</u> and <u>Lesson.</u> Select pages from the list of bookmarks to print out, which the children can use to decorate their poems.

Re-source

http://faculty.washington.edu/chudler/neurok.html

The Five Senses

What is it?_____

What do you see?	How does it feel?	How does it taste?	How does it smell?	Can you hear it?
_____	_____	_____	_____	_____
_____	_____	_____	_____	_____
_____	_____	_____	_____	_____
_____	_____	_____	_____	_____
_____	_____	_____	_____	_____
_____	_____	_____	_____	_____

I see _____

It feels _____

It tastes _____

It smells _____

I hear _____

It feels _____

It tastes _____

It smells _____

My Feelings

Key Words

happy, sad, angry, proud, clap, raise, stomp, stand

Subjects

music, language arts, physical education

Get Ready

• Preview and bookmark the Internet sites below for clip art and lyrics.

I

• Write the word *happy* and draw a big smiley face on the board. Give a big smile! Ask children to show you what they do when they're happy. Also talk about what they don't do.

B

• Form a circle. Model the first verse. Repeat it as necessary, encouraging the children to clap and sing.

> If you're **happy** and you know it, **clap your hands**.
> If you're **happy** and you know it, **clap your hands.**
> If you're **happy** and you know it, and you really want to show it,
> If you're **happy** and you know it, **clap your hands.**

• Go back. Make each verse cumulative. The children can show or tell other happy things they do. (Example: give a yell; jump up and down.) Add new words and actions to each line. Add a melody track.

A

• From time to time return to the song to introduce other feelings.

> If you're sad ... raise your hand.
> If you're angry ... stomp your feet.
> If you're proud ... stand up tall.

Re-source

http://www.webclipart.about.com/internet/webclipart/msubsmile.htm
Select from these links to galleries of emotions and smiley clip art. The Internet is packed with galleries of smiley faces to help talk about feelings. Use the illustrations for everything from prompts, bulletin board decorations, and making books on feelings.

http://www.northern-pine.com/songs/
Brooke's Sing-a-Song page provides a lively melody track and lyrics.

The Things I Eat

Key Words

names of foods, breakfast, lunch, dinner, snacks

Subjects

health, science, art, language arts

Get Ready

- Magazine, newspaper pictures of food; pictures from the Internet site below
- Art supplies for making mobiles (paper plates, 4 per child; wire clothes hangers; string)
- Preview the Internet site below. Download, print, and copy one of the food pyramids and pictures. Cut up the pyramid by food groups so that the children can put it together as a puzzle, 1 per child.

I
- Tell children they are going to build a food pyramid from the puzzle pieces you've distributed. As they work, they should call out the names of the foods they see. Talk about which of these foods they eat for breakfast, lunch, dinner, and for snacks. Explain that a healthy diet should contain foods from each group each day in the amounts listed on the pyramid.

I
- Connect to **http://www.usda.gov/news/usdakids/food_pyr.html**. Have children click on each food group and identify the foods.

B
- After your discussion of healthy eating and foods, which may go over several days, have children use 4 paper plates to make a collage for breakfast, lunch, dinner, and snacks. When completed, the collages can be strung to a wire hanger to make mobiles. Select foods from the pictures to make a classroom food pyramid.

Re-source

http://www.usda.gov/news/usdakids/food_pyr.html

The Things I Touch

Key Words

hard, soft, rough, smooth

Subjects

language arts, science

Get Ready

- Paper bags, small note cards for the scavenger hunt
- Choose items with a variety of textures and place each object in a paper bag. For example, *hard* (rock, nuts, and bolts); *soft* (cotton, crumpled tissue); *rough* (sandpaper, scrubbing pad, coral); *smooth* (plastic spoons, mirror, aluminum foil).
- Make a set of rebus cards from the reproducible below (one for each group).
- Preview the Internet site below to extend the activity.

I
- Tell children not to look in the bags that you pass around. Have them feel the objects and try to guess what each item might be. Supply the necessary adjectives and descriptive words.

B
- Show each of the rebus cards. Read it. Engage children in a discussion. For example, *This rock is hard. Name other things that are hard. What do you see around the room that's also hard?*

B
- Form pairs to go on a scavenger hunt around the room. Give each group a set of rebus cards. Tell them to look for things like those on the cards and put the items in the bags. If they find something too big to put in the bag, they should draw a picture of it. When the children return from the scavenger hunt, have them share their findings. Talk about what things have more than one quality. Some things, for example, might be both hard and smooth. Let children sort things as they talk about their qualities.

Re-source

http://www.fi.edu/qa97/me10/me10.html
The Franklin Institute of Science has information and activities on the sense of touch.

This [rock] is hard.	This [sandpaper] is rough.
This [cotton] is soft.	This [mirror] is smooth.

© 2001 Rigby

The Things I Do

Key Words

home, school, morning, afternoon, night, words to name personal hygiene, and daily activities

Subjects

health, social studies

Get Ready

- Props to demonstrate daily activities and personal hygiene, such as toothbrush and toothpaste, comb, spoon, book
- Chart paper
- Masking tape
- Reproducible 5, one for each child, and several cut up for classroom use.
- Preview the Internet site below for background.

B

- Use the props to pantomime and talk about things the children do at home and school to take care of themselves. Model simple sentences that tell what you are doing. For example, *I am eating my breakfast; I am combing my hair.* Then invite the children to follow your lead.

B

- Distribute the reproducible. Have the children talk about what they see. Categorize the activities using a Venn diagram. Draw it on chart paper. Label the left-hand circle *home;* the right-hand circle *school;* and the overlapping section *both.* Ask volunteers to tape a picture from the reproducible in the correct section as they talk about what they do at home and at school. Move the pictures as necessary.

home   both   school

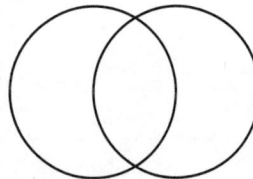

I

- Have the children draw their faces on the reproducible, then color and cut apart the frames. Use the pictures as prompts to help children learn about how they take care of themselves.
  - Sort the pictures into home and school activities, or by time of day.
  - Arrange the pictures in sequence.
  - Use the write-on lines for labeling and writing. Put the pictures together and make little books.

Re-source

http://www.kidshealth.org/

REPRODUCIBLE 5: THE THINGS I DO

✂

_____

_____

_____

_____

_____

_____

_____

_____

My Story

Key Words

title, author, illustration/picture, illustrator

Subjects

language arts, geography, social studies

Get Ready

- A favorite storybook with an easily readable title page.
- 12" x 18" or $8\frac{1}{2}$" x 11" white or colored paper, 3 sheets per child.
- Reproducible 6, one for each emergent reader.
- Write each of the sentence frames from Reproducible 6 on the board.
- Print out national flags from the Internet site below.

B

- Show the children a favorite storybook. Turn to the title page and refer to the book jacket to demonstrate key words such as *title, author, illustrator,* and *illustration.* Have volunteers point to an example of each word. Engage them in conversation as you ask questions to get at the meaning of the words *Who wrote the book? What is the title?*

I

- Tell children they are going to write a book about themselves called *My Story.* Show children how to make a Step Book. Give each child three sheets of paper. Line up the three sheets with approximately one-inch overlap on each one. Fold down the top sections of all three pages to form the step book. Staple across the top or use a hole punch and yarn to bind the books.

- Brainstorm types of important events and special interests in children's lives. For example: birthdays, new homes, sports, hobbies. Write them on the board and encourage the children to include them in their biographies.

B

- Go page by page. Title the first page *My Story* and have the child include his or her name. For children who are at the emergent stage, use the sentence frames from the reproducible on the next page. Model by providing information about yourself. Help the children fill out their sentence frames, cut, paste down, and illustrate each page. Children who are more fluent can create their own sentences.

Re-source

http://www.fotw.ca/flags/iso3166.html
Choose a country from the alphabetical list and click to see the flag.

I am ___ years old. My birthday is _____.

My address is _____.

I have ___ people in my family.

I am from _____.

This is the flag from my home country.

We've Got the Whole World

© 2001 Rigby

Key Words
globe, world, map, country(ies), ocean(s), continent(s), mountain(s), river(s)

Subjects
geography, music, language arts, physical education

Get Ready
- A classroom globe, world relief map (optional)
- A beach ball globe
- Preview and bookmark the Internet site below.

A • Connect to **http://hum.amu.edu.pl/~zbzw/glob/glob1.htm**. Show children several different views of the Earth. Select maps to help children identify *continents, oceans, mountains, rivers*. When possible, have the children identify their home countries. Print the pictures for classroom display. Make comparisons to the classroom globe and relief maps.

B • Form a circle and teach the verse.

We've got the whole world in our hands, (repeat 4 times)

When the children begin to join in, pass the globe from one child to the next. Whoever has the globe when the verse is finished, goes to the center of the circle. Begin the song again substituting his or her name. *Maria's got the whole world in her hands.* Children join hands and circle left. After children become familiar with the song, select other maps. Review land forms. Substitute *all the continents, oceans, mountains, rivers* for *whole world*.

I • Use the song to introduce and practice personal pronouns and possessive adjectives. For example, *She's got all the rivers in her hands.* Use props or pictures to pass around. Change the words to include such things as the earth's resources, the planets and stars, animals, people we care about.

Re-source
http://hum.amu.edu.pl/~zbzw/glob/glob1.htm
The Great Globe Gallery. Review the index and select maps that you find helpful.

Our Families

Key Words

family, brother, sister, mother, father, grandmother, grandfather, aunt, uncle, cousin

Subjects

social studies, art, language arts

Get Ready

- Art Supplies (crayons, markers, scraps of construction paper, scissors)
- Craft sticks
- Reproducible 7, one per child
- Preview and print out pictures from the Internet site below.

B

- As you show the children each of the family pictures from the Internet, encourage children to talk about who they think these people are, what they are doing, how they might be related to each other. Brainstorm names of other family members not shown (*aunt, uncle, grandmother, grandfather*). Invite children to use their native languages to name these family members, so that others in the class can become familiar with those words.

B

- Distribute the reproducible figures. Tell the children that they can make these figures into one or more family members—someone they live with or someone they feel close to. Have them cut, color, and decorate the figures. Have them glue a stick onto the back of each figure leaving enough room on the stick to hold the figure.

I

- Model a dialogue. Suggest such settings as birthday parties, outings, family visits, or meal time. Divide children into small groups to talk about these things with their figures. Monitor the discussions. Have children invent scenarios. Encourage dialogue both between a child's own figures and those of his or her classmate.

Re-source

http://www.yahooligans.com/Around_the_World/Regions/
This site provides pictures about families and their countries of origin.

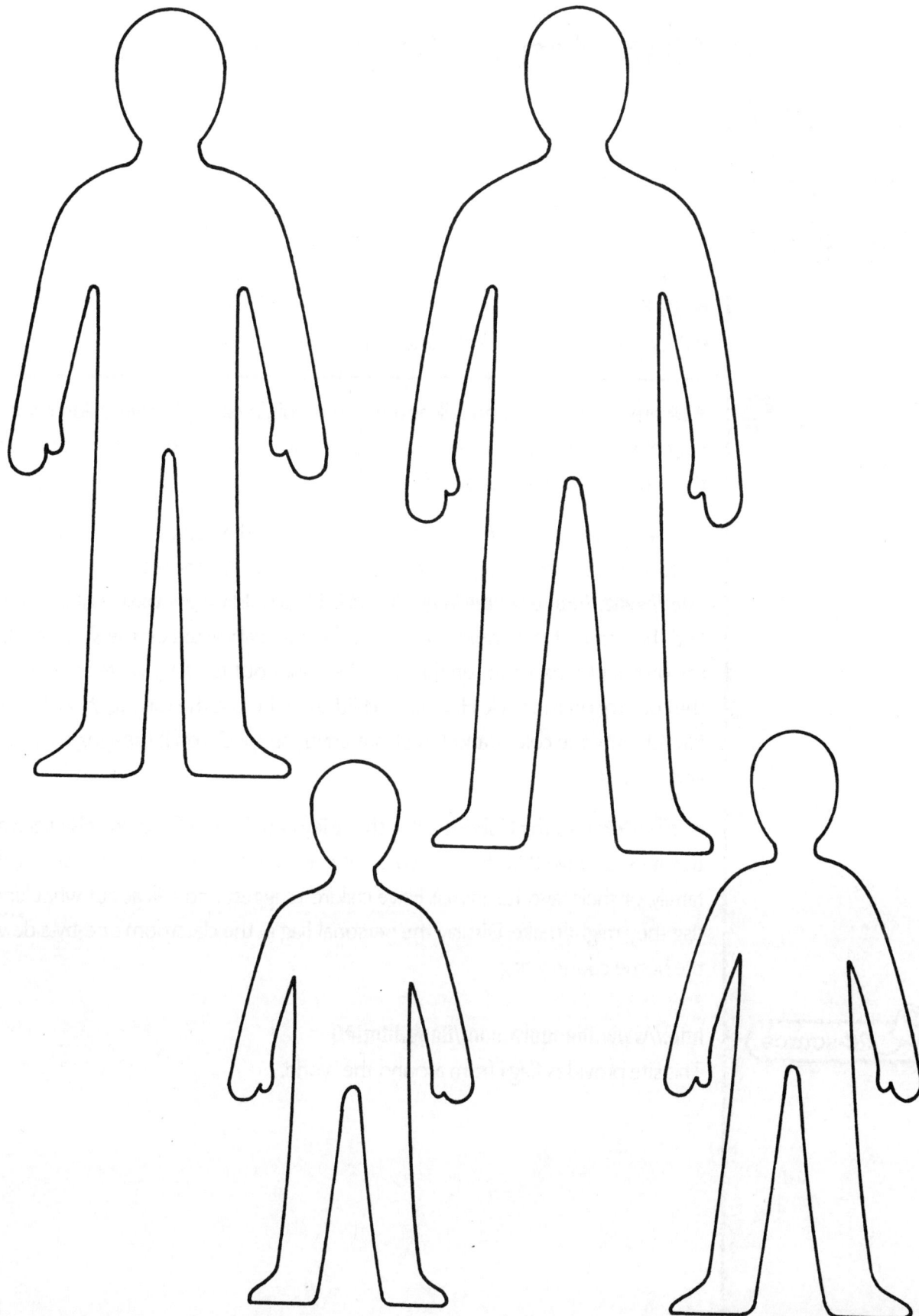

Our Home Countries

Key Words

flag, country, stars, stripes, color words

Subjects

social studies

Get Ready

- Sentence strips cut long enough to print the name of a country, one or more per student
- U.S. flag
- Preview and bookmark the Internet site below.

- Display the U.S. flag and talk about it (symbols, meaning). Have children identify the colors, stripes, and stars. Count the number of each. Help children understand that each country has its own flag.

- Have children name their home countries. List each country on the board and write it on a sentence strip to be given to that child. Connect to **http://www.theodora.com/flags.html#D**. Help children use their sentence strips to find the name of their home countries alphabetically listed on the Web site. Click on the country name to see the flag. Then print out the flag. Write the name of the country on the back. Have each child stand before the class to show his or her flag, identify the colors, and talk about anything special on it (designs, shapes, and symbols).

- Tell children to think about a flag that they could make for themselves. Suggest that it could have their favorite colors. It could have drawings of themselves, their family, or their favorite animal. Have children suggest and talk about what kind of flag they might make. Display the personal flag in the classroom side-by-side with the home country flag.

Re-source

http://www.theodora.com/flags.html#D
This site provides flags from around the world.

Where We Live

Key Words

street, house, apartment, big, small, tall, wide, narrow

Subjects

social studies, geography, art

Get Ready

- Art supplies (drawing paper, crayons, markers, scissors)
- Draw a street horizontally across the middle of a piece of mural paper.
- Wood blocks
- Yarn or string
- Preview and bookmark the Internet site below.

1
- Ask children to close their eyes and visualize the street where they live. To initiate discussion, use gestures to convey meaning as you ask how long is the street? How wide is it? Can you see buildings that are tall or small? Invite volunteers to use small blocks on a table to build various sized houses and apartment buildings to continue the discussion. Compare the size of buildings using words such as *bigger, smaller, taller, wide,* and *narrow.* Encourage children to join in the comparison.

B
- Ask children to draw a picture of their home. Encourage them to draw it in detail. Have them color and cut out their drawings. Glue the pictures on the mural paper on the wall. This will become the class "street." Brainstorm a name for the street and vote on it. Encourage volunteers to go up to the mural and point out their homes. Use the mural to reinforce language by having children point out the different colors and describe the sizes of the houses.

A
- Connect to **http://www.mapblast.com.** Type in the school's address. Print the map and point out areas near the school. (Note: there is a zoom-in function for added detail). Work with individuals to type in their addresses and print maps of their neighborhoods. Post the maps around the mural. (Check district policy before displaying children's personal information, and obtain required permissions.) Have children take string or yarn to connect their house on the mural to the map. Use this visual to model and practice survival language, giving names, addresses, and telling directions.

Re-source

http://www.mapblast.com

Our Neighborhood

Key Words
post office, bank, supermarket, hospital, school, restaurant

Subjects

social studies, language arts

Get Ready

- Collect realia from a hospital, bank, post office, supermarket, school, and restaurant (brochures, letterheads, ads, business cards, menus, shopping bags). Set up stations around the classroom for each of these businesses. Display a label naming the business and the realia at each station.
- Pictures of businesses, parks, and places of interest in your neighborhood
- Permission slips according to your district's policy for neighborhood visits
- Preview the Internet site below for background.

I
- Ask children what places they visit in the neighborhood. Show pictures as prompts. Show children the realia you have collected from places in the area. Ask if they can identify the things that they see. Go on a classroom walk to each of the stations. Ask children what people do in those places. Have children pantomime their responses while other children guess what they are doing.

I
- Have children form groups at each station and create a role-play for that location. For example, if the children choose to role-play a restaurant scene, they could make menus and act out what happens in the restaurant. Have each group share their role-play with the class. Practice dialogues such as *Do you have _____? I would like _____. Please. Thank you.*

A
- Go on a neighborhood visit to a facility near the school. Generate language by having children identify the place and tell about what happens there. If you have prearranged a visit, have the children ask questions. Collect other realia. Perhaps end up at a park or playground as a reward for lessons well learned.

Re-source

http://www.chamberfind.com
Locate your area's Chamber of Commerce and see if their Web site offers local maps, directories of local businesses, and pictures of local landmarks.

Our Relatives

Key Words

mother, father, aunts, uncles, cousins (and other family members),visit, run, jump, shout, kiss, hug, read, shake, eat, watch

Subjects

language arts, social studies, science

Get Ready

- Copy "My Family Visits Me" to use as a transparency or handout.
- Preview and bookmark the Internet site below to extend the activity.

I

- Display "My Family Visits Me" on an overhead or hand out copies to the children. Teach this finger play putting both hands up. Model each verse and encourage children to join in.

My Family Visits Me

I have ten cousins who come to visit me.	(fingers with faces)
We run.	(fingers running along in the air)
We jump.	(fingers hopping)
And we shout with glee.	(fingers closing and opening)
I have four aunts who come to visit me.	(two fingers on each hand)
We kiss.	(two fingers from each hand touching)
We hug.	(two fingers of each hand crossing)
Then they read to me.	(hands together like open book)
I have three uncles who come to visit me.	(two fingers and one finger)
We shake hands.	(hands shaking with each other)
We eat.	(eating motion with hand)
Sometimes we watch TV.	(finger circles in front of eyes)

Repeat finger play. Substitute numbers, relatives, and action words. For example, *I have one brother who comes to visit me./We play./We eat./And we shout with glee.*

A

- Once children have discussed their own families connect to **http://www.hbo4kids.com/shows/babar** to meet a cartoon elephant family. Use the pictures to compose a poem and finger play about an elephant family. It might be called, "When the Elephants Come to Visit."

Re-source

http://www.hbo4kids.com/shows/babar

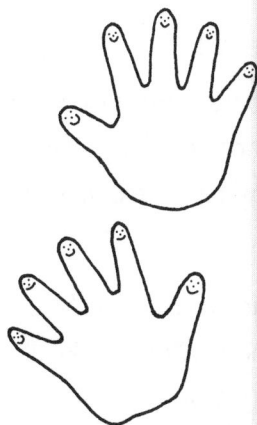

We Eat Rice All Over the World

Key Words

rice, grow, cook, brown, white

Subjects

social studies, geography, science, health

Get Ready

- Place samples of cooked brown and white rice on plates and label these. Have enough of each type so that each child may taste each. *Always check for food allergies before serving food to children.*
- If possible have rice cooking in a rice cooker during the activity.
- Small paper plates, bowls, and spoons
- Preview the Internet sites below for background, pictures, and recipes.

A

- Draw on children's experience. Encourage children to pantomime and describe how rice is cooked and eaten at home. Demonstrate and teach the necessary vocabulary, such as *pot, cover, boiling water,* and *simmer.* Introduce or review names for dinnerware and cutlery, such as *plate, knife, fork, spoon,* and *chopsticks.*

- Ask if children know where rice comes from before it gets to the store. How and where does it grow? Show pictures from the Internet sites of rice growing around the world. Refer to a globe or map to point out the countries where rice is grown (Thailand, Vietnam, U.S.).

- Serve small portions of cooked brown rice and white rice. Elicit responses about how each tastes, looks, smells, and feels. Make comparisons and contrasts. Take a class vote on which rice is preferred. Tally the results. Explain in simple language that brown and white rice are the same; the brown rice still has its hard outer layer.

Re-source

http://www.ricecafe.com/
http://www.irri.org.crucial.htm
Background, pictures, and recipes for rice

We Break Bread All Over the World

Key Words

bread, world, skinny, fat, round, flat

Subjects

language arts, health, social studies, geography

Get Ready

📕 *Bread Bread Bread* by Ann Morris, Mulberry Books, 1993.

📕 Additional book resource, *From Father to Son* by Pat Almada, Rigby Books, 1997

- A world map
- Removable adhesive dots
- A variety of breads (loaves, rolls, tortillas, flat breads)
- Sandwich fixings (peanut butter, jelly, cheese, lettuce, condiments)
- Kitchen utensils (breadboard, knives, cookie cutters)
- Preview and bookmark the Internet site below.

B • Before reading the book, look at the pictures. Ask the children to tell you what this book might be about. Encourage children to find and to talk about the pictures of breads and places that they recognize. Locate those places on the map and mark them with an adhesive dot. Read the story using your preferred guided reading strategies.

B • When you reread the story, use the words and/or pictures to play a bread game. Have the children pretend they're bread. Then have them act out the kind of bread they see in the picture. On command, they might be a skinny bread, a fat bread, a pretzel, a piece of toast popping up. Have children show and tell about other things that are like the breads they see (things that are skinny, fat, round, delicious, and so on).

I • Break bread together. Set up a sandwich factory. Depending on your resources, assign each child a role as a sandwich maker (cutter, spreader, assembler, and so on). Assemble a variety of sandwiches (fat ones, skinny ones, round ones). Invite another class in to join you for a sandwich party. Take photographs and make drawings, then write about it and share it with kids around the world in the International Children's cookbook at **www.b.shuttle.de/ml1000.**

Re-source

www.b.shuttle.de/ml1000
The International Children's Cookbook

http://www.upword.com/bread/home.html
Visit to find and share bread recipes.

My School

names of places at school

Key Words

Subjects

language arts, social studies, art

Get Ready

- Prepare large name cards for the school's rooms and places that you want the children to know.
- Camera
- Materials for making a big book (construction paper, large writing paper)
- Preview the Internet site below to extend the activity.

B

- Tour places in and around the school. At each stopping point hold up a name card for that place. Talk about what you do and see. Take a picture of that place, preferably an action shot that includes the children and school personnel. Point out unusual and specific things (a water fountain, playground equipment).

- Review and discuss the pictures and your tour before you make the big book. (You will probably need at least 24 hours to develop your film.)

- Paste each picture on a large sheet of paper. Label each page with its name card. Have small groups illustrate and write or dictate sentences for each page. Put the pages together in a big book. Make a cover and decide on a title. Keep the book in the learning center. Refer to it to start discussions about directions, activities, and the people in and around school.

Re-source

http://www.yahooligans.com/School_Bell/School_Sites/
Visit some schools around the world.

My Classroom

Key Words

desk, chair, table, book, pencil, pen, crayon, paper, ruler, computer, scissors, globe, backpack

Subjects

all school subjects

Get Ready

- Prepare word and picture cards from Reproducible 8, one set for each pair of children. Select words you want the children to know and place these in a paper bag.
- Prepare label/flash cards for each of the words.
- Preview and bookmark the Internet site below.

B
- Show the flash cards you've selected. Help children identify the word and place it near that classroom object.

I
- Go on a classroom walk. Move from object to object. Talk about how to use the classroom object. Encourage children to act out using or working with it.

- Model a guessing game in which you describe the word and have the children point out and guess the object. When the children have mastery of the words, have them sit in pairs with their backs to each other. Take turns. One child picks a word/picture card from the bag and describes and talks about it to his partner. (Remind them not to say the word.) The other partner writes the word or draws it.

A
- Have the children visit classrooms around the world. Encourage them to talk about what they see. When possible select sites that represent your children's home countries. Go to **yahooligans.com/School_Bell/School_Sites/**. Select a country. Go to sites that show pictures of kids at school in that country.

Re-source

http://www.yahooligans.com/School_Bell/School_Sites/

desk	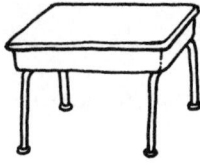	paper	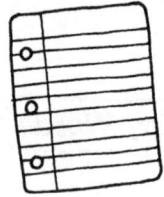
chair		ruler	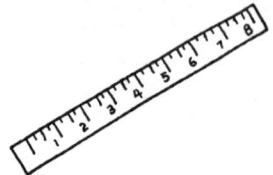
table	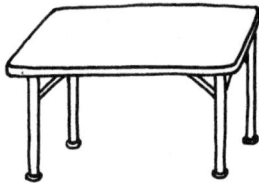	computer	
book		scissors	
pencil	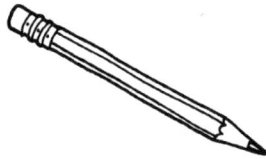	globe	
pen	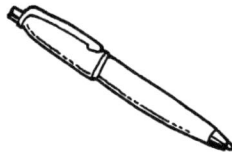	backpack	
crayon		clock	

Speaking and Listening Together

Key Words

talking stick, discussion, Native American, equality

Subjects

social studies, history, language arts

Get Ready

- An 8" to 12" stick, large feathers and pieces of fur to decorate it (optional decorations might include beads, yarn leather)
- Go to **http://www.americanwest.com/pages/genres.htm** for links to useful Native American Web sites. Go to **http://www.geocities.com/rainforest/9637/pg000014.htm** to see a picture of an authentic talking stick.

A

- With the children visit the Internet sites you've chosen. Talk about the tradition of the Talking Stick. Explain that at meetings, the elder would hold the Talking Stick and speak first, then hold out the Talking Stick to anyone else who wished to speak. Whoever held it could speak without interruption. The eagle feather on the stick gave courage and wisdom to speak truthfully; the rabbit fur reminded the speaker to speak from the heart. Elicit examples of *speaking truthfully* and *from the heart.*

  As a group, make a Talking Stick. Include a large feather and a small piece of fur as they represent traditional parts of the Talking Stick.

- Decide on a topic of current interest (school rules, safety, a subject area). Gather children in a circle on the floor and explain these rules for the Talking Stick:

  - Listen to the speaker. Try not to think about what you are going to say.
  - Anyone can "pass" the stick without speaking.
  - Don't comment on or judge what classmates have said. Just speak from your own heart.
  - Observe a few seconds of silence between speakers.

- Incorporate the Talking Stick strategy to discuss class issues and problems, conflict resolution, reviewing content material, introducing a new subject, doing role-plays, or discussing feelings without personalizing.

Re-source

http://www.geocities.com/rainforest/9637/pg000014.htm
See a picture and brief description of an Indian talking stick.

http://www.americanwest.com/pages/genres.htm
Visit site to find Native American resources.

Work Song

Key Words reading, writing, science, math, history, social studies, art, words for work

Subjects social studies, language arts

Get Ready

Worksong written by Gary Paulsen, illustrated by Ruth Wright Paulsen, Harcourt Brace, 2000.
- Paper or index cards, two per child
- Preview and bookmark the Internet site below.

I

- Preview the cover and pictures. Encourage children to identify the workers and what they are doing. Ask children what other kinds of jobs people do. List those on a word bank. Before reading, tell children to think about the kinds of work that they would like to do. Read the story using your preferred guided reading strategies. Have the children act out the pictures.

A

- Go to **http://stats.bls.gov/k12/html/edu_over.htm**. Look at the homepage icons. Work with children to identify these icons as representing school subjects. Have children name and point to similar things in the classroom to make the associations. Help them understand that people often use what they learn at school to help them at work. Click on each icon of a school subject to go to pictures of people who use those school subjects at work. Use these pages to help children identify people at work. (The pictures may also be printed out and used as word/picture cards.)

A

- Give the children two sheets of paper or index cards. On one have them draw and label a picture of themselves at a job they would like to do. On the other have them draw an icon or picture of the school subject(s) that would help them do that work. Display each child's pair of drawings on the bulletin board. Work with children to talk about and rearrange the pictures. Cluster pictures of similar jobs and the subject areas that help those people at work. Then choose pictures. Work as a class or in small groups to have the children talk about and match the school subject icons to the work that is shown.

Re-source

http://stats.bls.gov/k12/html/edu_over.htm
Bureau of Labor Statistics site with school-to-work connections

Our Community at Work

Key Words

words for stores and businesses

Subjects

social studies, geography, language arts

Get Ready

- Collect newspaper ads and advertising supplements for local stores and businesses. Select four or five ads with pictures and words that show people at work, their products, and services.
- Scissors
- Preview and bookmark the Internet site below.

I

- Gather the children so they can see each ad that you display. Invite children to talk about what they see. Work together to associate each ad with a place of business. List the businesses or stores on the the board. Going business by business, encourage children to visualize each place. Generate language by modeling sentences, such as *I go/went to the community bookstore. I buy/bought books and magazines. I see/saw a table with books. I see/saw a computer.* Under each business, list the things associated with that place of work. Suggest other places.

<u>Bank</u>   <u>Supermarket</u>   <u>Candy Store</u>   <u>Department Store</u>

A

- Go to **http://www.anywho.com** Select <u>Find Businesses</u> to search the business name in the ad. Point out and review addresses and telephone numbers. Select <u>Maps</u> that you can zoom in and out for detail. Compare these maps with the map you've printed with the location of your school. Some businesses may have home pages to give you more information and pictures about your community at work.

A

- Have the children work in small groups. Distribute additional newspapers and advertising supplements. Have the children cut out ads for businesses and identify the places of work. As a group, share information. Name the businesses, their products, and services.

- Play a phonics game. Select words to teach and practice initial consonants, consonant clusters, and digraphs. For example, ask children what they can find at the community bookstore, that begins with /b/, at the supermarket that starts with /c/.

Re-source

http://www.anywho.com
Enter your school name or a nearby address and print out a map. Select <u>zoom</u> for detail.

People at Work

Key Words

names of people at work; wh words

Subjects

social studies, language arts

Get Ready

- Invite people (school personnel, parents, community liaisons, especially police officers and firefighters) to come to your classroom to talk about their work. Invite enough people so that the children can work in small groups with one of the visitors. Ask them to bring along work-related props and realia. Ask for and record your visitors' email addresses at work.
- The questionnaire on Reproducible 9, one per student, and one per group
- Preview the Internet site below for background.

- Prior to meeting your classroom visitors, tell children that they will meet people who do many kinds of work. Brainstorm things they would like to know about those people and the work they do. Introduce the questionnaire. Familiarize the children with each question. Practice having them fill out a sample questionnaire using yourself as the model. Go over procedures and language for welcoming and introducing the visitors.

- Introduce the visitors. Assign small groups of children to each visitor. Have them use the questionnaire to find out about their visitor's job. In the remaining class time, have each group introduce the visitor and let the visitor talk about his/her work with a question/answer session.

- In a subsequent class, review and summarize the questionnaires and talk about your visitors' jobs. Show the class your Internet email service. Work with the class to create a thank you note for the visitors to email to them at their workplace.

Re-source

http://stats.bls.gov/K12/html/edu_over.htm

http://home.nycap.rr.com/cjem/ems
Visit for information on careers and occupations.

Name:

_____

Email address:

_____

Where do you work?

_____

_____

When do you work?

_____

_____

What do you do?

_____

_____

What do you like best about your work?

_____

_____

_____

_____

_____

_____

_____

_____

The More We Work Together

Key Words

work, play, get together, friends, happier

Subjects

music, physical education, language arts

Get Ready

- Preview the Internet site below for lyrics to the song "The More We Get Together"
- This song and dance need space to move around. Go outdoors if weather permits.

- Talk about times the children work together in class or with their family. Prompt them with questions. *What do you do? How do you feel? Do you feel happy, sad, busy?* List responses. Teach the song "The More We Get Together" incrementally. Build it two lines two at a time. Sing it and have the children repeat. To vary the practice, divide the class into two groups and have them alternate lines or verses.

- Refer to the song. Brainstorm words that the children can substitute for *get together (work, play, laugh together)*. Have them act it out. Elaborate on the meaning of *happy* and *happier* in the song. Draw from the children's experience to elicit responses. For example, you might ask, *Would one piece of candy make Doris happy? Would two pieces of candy make Muhammed happier?* Brainstorm other comparative adjectives that can be substituted in the song for *happier (funnier, nicer, noisier, crazier, smarter)*. Sing the song again, substituting different words for *work* and *happier*.

The more we <u>work</u> together, together, together,
The more we <u>work</u> together, the happier we'll be.

For your friends are my friends and my friends are your friends,
The more we <u>work</u> together, the happier we'll be.

Re-source

http://rididdles.com/mouseum/m010.html
Lyrics for "The More We Get Together"

• Add movement and dance. Form two concentric circles, one inside the other, with children facing inside. Join hands.

Movements for first two lines:
Outside circle move to the right.
Inside circle move to the left.
Stop at the end and face partners.
Hold hands.
Skip in a circle.

Movements for second two lines:
Stand in place.
Point to partner for "your friends."
Point to self for "my friends.
Hold hands and skip in a circle with partner for the last lines of the second verse.

• Repeat with word substitutions. For example, *the more we laugh together, the funnier we'll be.*

Animals Work Together, Too

Key Words
ants, nest, colony, community, workers, queen, males, females, larvae, pupae

Subjects
science, social studies, language arts

Get Ready

- Magnifying lens
- Go to **http://ant.edb.miyakyou.ac.jp/INTRODUCTION/Gakken79E/Page_02. html.** Select from the Table of Contents <u>Ant nest</u>; <u>Ant family</u>, <u>Ant eggs, larvae and pupae</u>. Choose pictures and activities from any of these kid-friendly pages to illustrate the lives of ants working together. Select pictures to print out. Reproduce a picture of an ant colony, one per child.
- Reproducible 10, word/picture cards, one set per child
- A classroom table to serve as an ant nest
- Preview and bookmark the Internet sites listed below.

A

- Observe ant life live at **http://ant.edb.miyakyo-u.ac.jp/INTRODUCTION/ Gakken79E/Page_02.html** or **http://www.school.discovery.com/homeworkhelp/ worldbook/atozscience/a/ 023560.html** or in an ant colony. Shelter the English. For example, *These are ants at work. They live in a nest. These are the larvae. Soon they will turn to pupae.* While small groups of children observe the ants, click and drag from one page to another, ask questions such as, *Where have you seen ants? What color are they? Which way are they moving?* List their comments.

- Give children a picture of an ant colony or nest and a set of picture cards. Display the picture cards and identify the *queen, eggs, males, workers, larvae,* and *pupae.* As you discuss ants at work, have the children manipulate the picture cards around the printout of the nest. Ask children to volunteer to place the cutouts in different parts of the nest. Fill in the spaces around the cutouts with tunnels and alcoves.

- Use a large classroom table as the nest. Have children crawl under the table, around and through it as they role-play life in an ant colony. Pick roles. Allow children to work together to form a skit. Give suggestions and prodding as needed.

Re-source

http://ant.edb.miyakyo-u.ac.jp/INTRODUCTION/Gakken79E/Page_02.html
This site describes how to build an ant colony

http://www.school.discovery.com/homeworkhelp/worldbook/atozscience/a/ 023560.html

nest

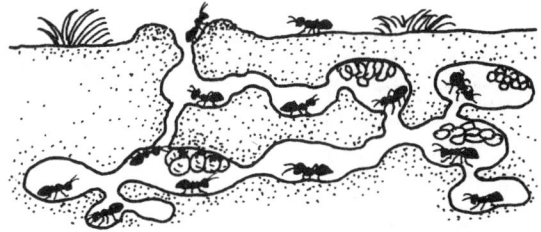

workers

queen

males

larvae

pupae

In Case of Emergency

Key Words

home, work, police, fire, doctor, ambulance, poison

Subjects

social studies, health, language arts

Get Ready

- Prepare an overhead and/or display of the emergency numbers located on the first page of the telephone directory.
- Reproduce the emergency numbers (below) and paste down on an index card, one per student.
- Play telephone with phones the children can make from paper cups and strings.
- Preview the Internet site below for additional safety information.

- Familiarize the children with the emergency telephone numbers listed in the telephone directory. Talk about emergency situations.

- Work together to fill in the emergency numbers below. Use information on file to fill in the family telephone numbers or, if necessary, have the child take it home.

- Model conversations so that the children know who to call and what to say in case of emergency: *I need help. My name is… I live at… My telephone number is…* Suggest an emergency and have the children work in pairs to role-play making telephone calls to the correct emergency numbers.

Re-source

www.yahooligans.com/Science_and_Nature/Health_and_Safety/Safety/
Links to safety information.

Emergency Numbers

Name _____

Family _____

Home _____

Work _____

Police _____

Fire _____

Doctor _____

Ambulance _____

Poison Control _____

From the Country to the City

Key Words

country, city, same, different

Subjects

social studies, geography, language arts

Get Ready

📖 *The Little House* by Virginia Lee Burton, Houghton Mifflin Co., 1978 (Winner of the Caldecott Medal.) Available in audiocassette.
- Masking tape or string
- Drawing paper
- Preview and bookmark the Internet sites below.

B
- Use masking tape or string to go down the middle of the room to divide it in half. Have the children walk around one side of the room and then the other, telling them to look and even listen to what is the same and what is different. List their responses under the headings: ***Same***   ***Different***

I
- Tell children that the story *The Little House* is about both the city and the country. When they look at the pictures and read the story they should look and listen for things that are the same and different, just as they did when they looked at the classroom. Preview the story by selecting several pairs of consecutive pictures. Have the children tell you what is the same and what is different in each set of pictures. Then have the children predict what the story is about. Read the book using your preferred guided reading strategy appropriate to the language level of your children.

B
- Distribute the drawing paper. Have the children draw pictures of their homes. Have them exchange their drawing with a classmate. Then have them tell what is the same and different about each. Children can also compare and contrast their drawings to pictures of places from around the world.

Re-source

http://www.yahooligans.com/downloader/pictures/places_to_see
Links to pictures from around the world

http://libweb.uoregon.edu/speccoll/mss/childrenslit/vlburton.html
Biographical and background information on author Virginia Lee Burton

Songs on Wheels and Wings

Key Words — transportation, train, bus, boat, airplane, car, bike, taxi

Subjects — history, social studies, music

Get Ready —
- Collect materials for making transportation toys (small boxes, milk cartons, paper tubes, spools).
- Gather art supplies (construction paper, paints, scissors, glue)
- Preview and bookmark the Internet sites below.

1
- Brainstorm ways children can travel in the city and country. Invite them to act out visiting city and country places by plane, train, car, bus, and bike. Ask children what they see.

A
- Take an online tour of transportation. Go to **www.airmuseum.org.** Select Planes and Exhibits. Go to **www.hfmgv.org** (The Henry Ford Museum). Select Online Exhibits. Go to **www.dgbn.com/train** (The Baltimore and Ohio Railroad Museum). Go to **www.ccg-gcc.gc.ca/** (The Canadian Coast Guard). Select Photos, Fact, History and more! Spend individual class periods exploring the history and types of transportation. Print out pictures.

A
- Provide children with materials and art supplies. Have them use the pictures from their online tour to make transportation toys. Encourage them to share information as they work. Teach the children transportation songs to accompany role-play using their toy vehicles. Go to **www.judyanddavid.com.** Select Songbook. Click on alphabetical listing for favorite transportation songs. (For example, "Wheels on the Bus," "Row, Row, Row Your Boat," "I've Been Working on the Railroad")

Re-source —
www.airmuseum.org

www.hfmgv.org

www.dgbn.com/train

www.ccg-gcc.gc.ca/

www.judyanddavid.com/

The City

Key Words

morning, evening, city, song

Subjects

language arts, social studies, geography

Get Ready

- Get a copy of "City," a poem by Langston Hughes. It is often reproduced in primary and elementary textbooks. It also can be found in ***The Random House Book of Poetry for Children***, selected by Jack Prelutsky. Random House: New York, 1983, pg. 98, or in other Langston Hughes poetry collections.
- Preview the Internet sites below for background.

1

- Pass around the city pictures. Allow children time to examine them. Have them identify what they know. Point out morning and evening scenes. Discuss and act out what the children do in the morning and at night.

- Tell children you would like to read them a poem about the city in the morning and the city at night. Ask children to close their eyes. Read the poem several times.

- Have children open their eyes. Check for understanding. Going line by line, encourage children to tell and act out what they heard. Have them ask questions about difficult words. Have children memorize the poem. Prepare a choral reading and add appropriate gestures (for example, when they say "spreads its wings" they might open their arms and spread them like wings).

Re-source

http://local.yahoo.com
Select your state, then select the big city closest to you. Go to city home pages and historical museums. Download pictures.

http://falcon.jmu.edu/~ramseyil/hughes.htm
Biographical and background information on author Langston Hughes.

Also search the Web by the name of a big city in your geographical area.

The Country

Key Words

names of farm animals, farm, farmer, barn, tractor, field

Subjects

social studies, language arts

Get Ready

- Display farm pictures
- One sentence strip per group with the following sentence frame:
  In the country we see _____.
- 7–10 index cards (as needed)
- Art supplies (markers, crayons)
- Download and print out pictures of farms and farm animals from the Internet sites below.

B

- View the pictures of farms with children. Help them name the things they see. Focus on the key words.

- Introduce the sentence strip.

> In the country we see _____

Brainstorm ideas on how to complete the sentence strips.

- Arrange children in different groups. Distribute one sentence strip to each group and three to four index cards. Refer to the farm pictures. Have each group decide what farm item they will draw on each index card to complete the sentence strip. (Example: *In the country we see a barn. In the country we see the cow.*) Help children label each drawing. Staple these word/picture cards to the right-hand corner of the sentence strip to make the sentence strip book. Place the sentence strip books in the reading center to be used for independent and partner work.

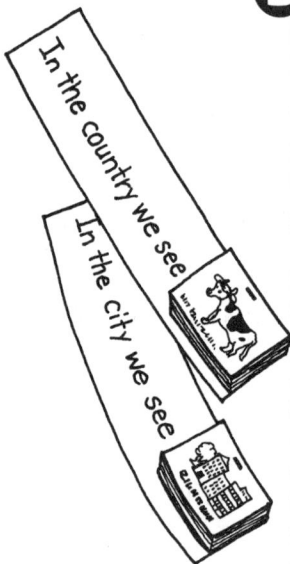

Re-source

http://www.turnaltfarm.co.uk/
Photographs of animals and scenes from a farm in Scotland

http://www.kidsfarm.com/farm.htm
Pictures of farm animals

http://www.yahooligans.com
Search under subject <u>farm</u> for pictures of the country.

In the City/In the Country

Key Words

city, country, both, pig, playground, traffic, apartment building, skyscraper, barn, bus, subway, house, cornstalk, cat, garden, stop sign

Subjects

social studies, language arts

Get Ready

- Reproducible 11 (picture cards), one sheet per student
- Reproducible 12, one per student
- Art supplies (drawing paper, crayons, markers)
- Preview the Internet site below for background.

B
- Distribute the sheet of picture cards. Identify and discuss each picture. Use TPR (Total Physical Response) commands to help children decide where they see these things. For example: *What is this?* (Traffic). *Raise your right hand if you see traffic in the city. Raise your left hand if you see traffic in the country. Raise both hands if you see traffic in the city and the country.*

B
- Distribute Reproducible 12. Ask children to cut apart the picture cards and display them. Have children follow your oral instructions.

  1. What do you find only in the country? Put those pictures under the barn.

  2. What do you find only in the city? Put those pictures under the skyscraper.

  3. What do you find both in the city and in the country? Put those pictures in the middle. (Remind children they can move things around.)

B
- Have volunteers share their work. Discuss their choices. Make necessary corrections and have children color and paste the pictures in place.

I
- Use the reproducible to model dialogue for classroom and partner discussion. For example: *In the country there are barns, but not in the city. In the city, there are skyscrapers, but not in the country. They have playgrounds in the city and the country.*

Re-source

http://www2.kenyon.edu/projects/famfarm/life/tier2.htm
Learn about life on a family farm.

Put the pictures in the right place.

Country	Both	City

Food From the Farm

Key Words

grow, farm, can, box, package, names of food, names of vegetables, names of fruit

Subjects

social studies, geography, language arts

Get Ready

- Collect a variety of packaged food (canned vegetables and fruit, dairy and juice containers, bread and wheat products).
- Art supplies (poster paper, markers, crayons, scissors, paste)
- Preview the Internet sites below to download and print out pictures and images.

B

- Display the packaged goods. Help children identify each one. Point out identifying words on the package (Example: milk, flour, orange juice).

A

- Help children link the package goods to where they came from on the farm. Ask questions. For example: *Who makes this? Where does this come from?*

I

- Distribute pictures downloaded from the Internet sites. Have children match the farm animal, plant, or produce to its packaged good. Have children color individual pictures. Paste each one on a separate sheet of poster paper. Cut labels from the packaged goods. Have children match them to the picture on the poster page and glue them near the matching picture. Put the pages together into a big book. Continue to add to the big book. Ask children to bring in package labels from foods they eat at home. Identify them and help identify where they come from on the farm. Print blackline clip art from the Internet sites that children can add to their big book.

Re-source

http://agpublications.tamu.edu/clipart/
Search <u>Keywords</u>: «enter name of animal, plant, or produce.» Choose words that correspond to each packaged good. (Example: *wheat* for flour.) Download pictures. Note: This site has hundreds of high quality blackline images that can be printed out for children to color or to use as picture references.

http://www.iband.com/clipart.html
Click on food and drink to download color images.

The Suburbs

Key Words

in, on, over, under, between, at, next to, across

Subjects

language arts, social studies

Get Ready

- Reproducible 13, one per child
- Classroom realia, books, pencils, other classroom objects to use for hands-on demonstration of the prepositions.

B
- Arrange the realia on your desk and throughout the room. Give TPR (Total Physical Response) commands to demonstrate and have the children use the objects to demonstrate the prepositions *in, on, over, under, between, at, next to, across.* For example: *Put the candy* **on** *the desk. Put the candy* **in** *your mouth.*

I
- Distribute the reproducible. Have the children cut apart the picture pieces as they identify the objects. Ask the children to follow your oral directions to complete the reproducible.

My name is Pedro. I live in the suburbs. Let me show you around.
1. Put Pedro next to the front door.
This is my house. I live at 354 Hope Street.
2. Put the numbers over the door.
3. Put the flowers under the window.
4. Put the bike between the two houses.
5. Put the car in the garage.
This is my neighborhood.
6. Put the mailbox on the corner.
7. Put the stop sign across the street.
8. Put the ball in the park.
9. Put the girl next to the swing.
Welcome to my neighborhood. Come visit!

I
- Review the work with the children. Have them paste down the picture pieces and color the reproducible. Use it to do a finger walk around the neighborhood as you give oral commands for directions using prepositions. Have the children work in partners to continue as you have modeled.

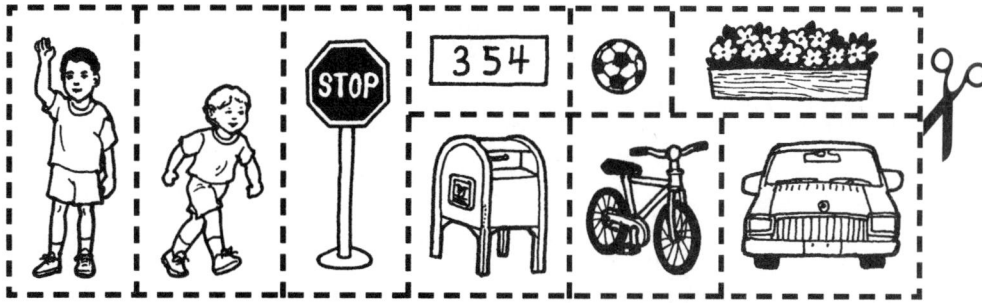

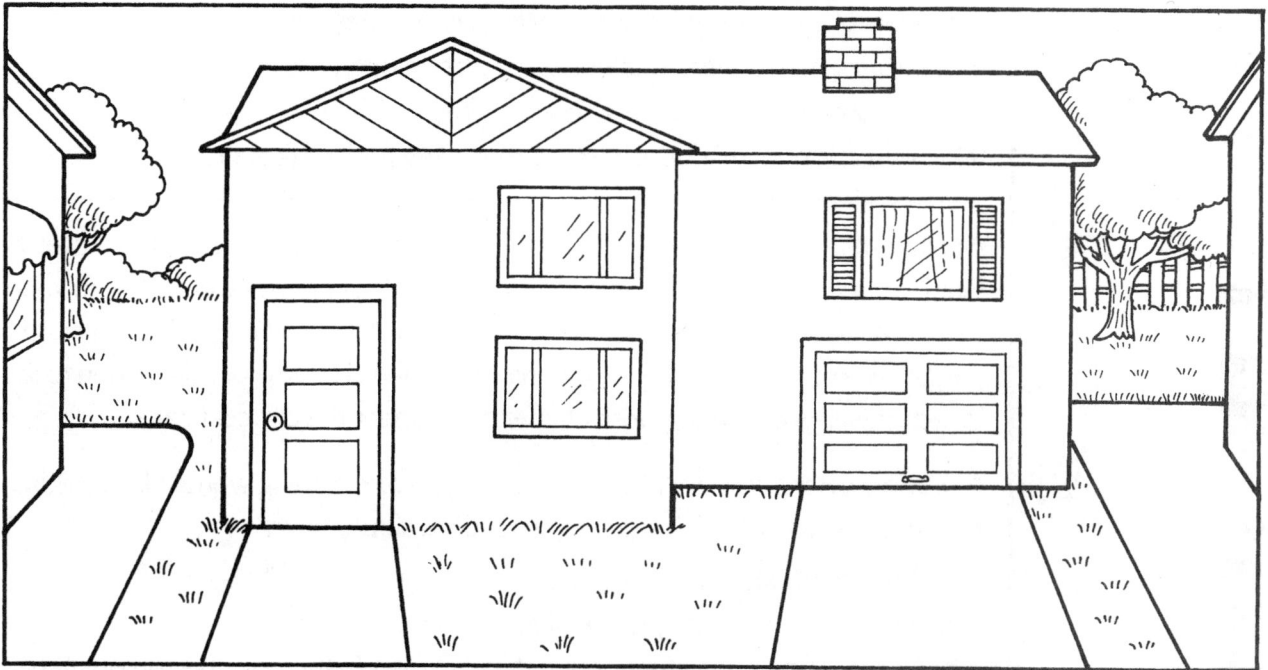

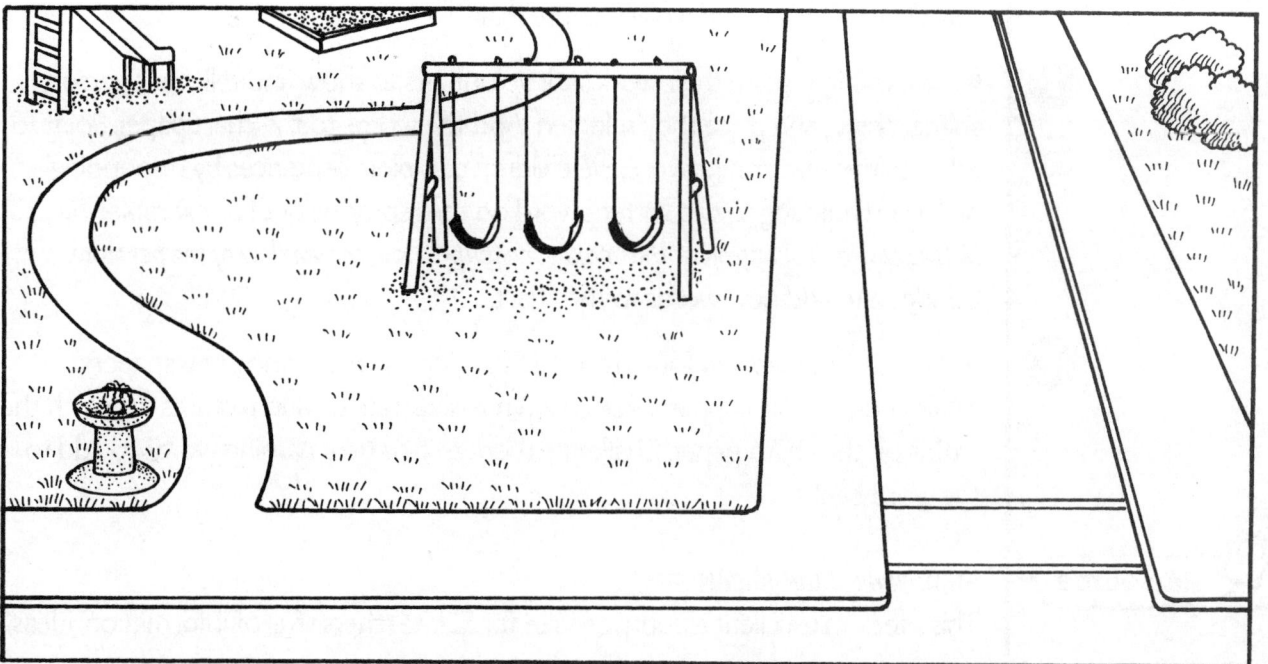

A Trip to the Mall

Key Words

mall, people, person, animal, place, thing

Subjects

social studies, art, language arts

Get Ready

- Reproducible 14, one per student
- 4 sheets of chart paper labeled: *people, animals, places, things*
- Magazines, newspapers, catalogues for picture references
- Art supplies (crayons, markers, scissors, glue)
- Preview and bookmark the Internet site below for background.

I

- Point out and read the headers on each sheet of chart paper. Tell children that the words *people, animals, places,* and *things* are four kinds of naming words. Ask children to think about the last time they went to the mall. Ask: *What did you see? What did you do?* As you discuss the trip to the mall, select words from your discussion to list in each category of naming words. Write them under the correct headers.

B

- Distribute Reproducible 14. Help children generate naming words. Have children use pencils as you read the following directions aloud.

  1. Draw a circle around a person.
  2. Draw a line under the picture of an animal.
  3. Draw an X on the picture of one thing you see that is not a person or animal.
  4. Draw a box around a place at the mall.

I

- Have children share their work. Ask volunteers to show and tell what person, animal, thing, and place they selected. Add the words to the chart paper. Point to other things that are shown. Have children complete sentences by responding orally and pointing to the correct word on the reproducible. For example: *This is a picture of people shopping at the (mall) . The (puppy) is in the window of the pet store.* Continue to add new words to the charts.

I

- Have children work in four groups. Distribute the magazines, newspapers, catalogues, and art supplies. Ask children to illustrate or find pictures to match the words on the chart paper. Challenge them to find new naming words to add to the word banks.

Re-source

http://www.englishclub.net/

This site is an excellent all-purpose site for ELL teachers–full of information, ideas, resources, and links.

Sounds on the Farm

Key Words

names of farm animals, (animal sounds)

Subjects

language arts, science, social studies, music, geography

Get Ready

- Preview and bookmark the Internet sites. Download and printout pictures for animals that you want children to name.

B

- Display the pictures of farm animals. Identify their names in English. Ask volunteers to tell what sound each animal makes. Begin with something easy such as a cow saying "moo" or a chick saying "peep." Distinguish individual sounds. Write them on the board and help the children sound them out.

I

- Connect to **http://www.georgetown.edu/cball/animals/**. Select <u>animals</u>. Click on the name of an animal. Look at the picture. Click on the sound icon to hear the animal sound. Start with languages spoken by your children. Point out the sound that animal makes in the chosen language. Encourage children to sound out the word with you. (Example: Spanish: *muuu.*) Explore and practice initial consonants, vowel sounds, and final sounds.

I

- Play a game of "Old MacDonald." Substitute the names and sounds of animals you have displayed and learned. Have volunteers name the animal and sound in their native language and alternate verses including home languages.

Re-source

http://www.kidsfarm.com/farm.htm

http://www.georgetown.edu/cball/animals/

YOUNG FASHION
B·E·S·T P·I·Z·Z·A
TACO
FROZEN YOGURT
FLAVORS
SALE
THEATER I · II · III
THEATER I
PETS

Singing Numbers

Key Words
thumb, shoe, knee, door, side, sticks, heaven, gate, spine, numbers 1-10

Subjects
music, language arts

Get Ready
- Reproducible 15, one copy per student
- Preview and download the number chart from the Internet site below.

1

- Teach "This Old Man" by singing each verse and having children repeat the verse along with actions.

This Old Man

This old man, he played <u>one</u>	(hold up one finger)
He played knick-knack <u>on my thumb</u>	(hold up thumb)
With a knick-knack, paddy whack	(clap hands)
Give a dog a bone	(pretend to throw a bone over your shoulder)
This old man came rolling home.	(make rolling motion with hands)

<u>two</u>	<u>shoe</u>	<u>five</u>	<u>side</u>	<u>eight</u>	<u>gate</u>
<u>three</u>	<u>knee</u>	<u>six</u>	<u>sticks</u>	<u>nine</u>	<u>spine</u>
<u>four</u>	<u>door</u>	<u>seven</u>	<u>up to heaven</u>	<u>ten</u>	<u>hen</u>

- Hand out the reproducible and have children identify the pictures and numbers. Children color and cut the cards.

- Pair children with partners and play a memory game. Place one set of picture and number cards face down. Have children take turns turning over two cards to match the number that rhymes with the picture. It is important that children be very familiar with the song before they play this game so it will not be too difficult.

Re-source

http://www.englishclub.net/handouts/vocabulary/cardinals_ordinals.htm
Provides a list of cardinal and ordinal numbers.

http://www.judyanddavid.com
Hear "This Old Man" by choosing the online songbook.

one		six	
two		seven	
three	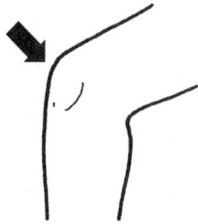	eight	
four		nine	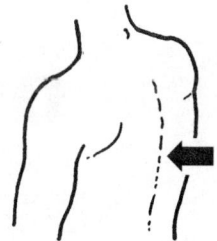
five		ten	

One to Ten

Key Words → the numbers 1-10; Can you tell me _____; Can you say _____; the names of the languages spoken in your classroom

Subjects → math, language arts, geography

Get Ready →
- A world map or globe
- Preview the Internet site below for additional information.

B
- Write the numbers 1–10 on the board, as the children count along. If you have a child in your class who speaks Cantonese, have the child count to 10 in Cantonese when you point to each number. Introduce the poem, "One to Ten." Ask the Chinese child to join in as you read the poem, otherwise refer to the numbers on the board as you say them in Cantonese.

> One to Ten, by Janet S. Wong*
>
> *Yut yee sam see*
> Count in Cantonese with me!
>
> *Eun look chut bot*
> Can you tell me what we've got?
>
> *Gow sup.* One to ten!
> Could you say that once again?

Generate other language using the sentence frames:
Can you tell me _____?   Could/Can you say _____?

* Reprinted with the permission of Margaret K. McElderry Books, an imprint of Simon and Schuster Children's Publishing Division from *Good Luck Gold and Other Poems* by Janet S. Wong. Copyright © 1994 Janet. S. Wong.

I
- Take a survey. How many languages are spoken in your classroom? Make a graph. Find places on a map or globe where those languages are spoken. Have children point out their home countries. Identify the place on the map with the child's name written on a self-adhesive note.

- Invite children to substitute the numbers 1-10 using their primary language. Adapt the verses to keep the rhythm. For example: *Uno dos tres cuatro, Count in Spanish, will you please?*

Re-source → **http://www.aaamath.com/cnt.html**
This site provides an interactive explanation with practice and wonderful games about counting.

One Hundred Is a Family

© 2001 Rigby

Key Words → the numbers 1-10; numbers for counting by tens through one hundred

Subjects → math, social studies, language arts

Get Ready → *One Hundred is a Family* by Pam Muñoz Ryan, illustrated by Benrei Huang, Hyperion Books for Children, 1996.
- Prepare a bar graph on chart paper, titled "People in Our Family." In the left-hand column, write the numbers 1–10. Fill in the grid to 15 spaces across.
- Reproducible 16 , one per child
- Art supplies (markers, crayons, scissors, yarn, string, buttons, fabric scraps)
- Preview the Internet site below for additional activities.

B
- Write the following numbers on the board:

  1 2 3 4 5 6 7 8 9 10 20 30 40 50 60 70 80 90 100

  Teach or review the numbers. Go number by number. Ask children to raise their hands if that is the total number of people in their family at home. Tabulate the count. Use the data to make a bar graph with each box on the grid representing one child's family. As you get to the higher numbers, draw children into the reading by telling them that even 100 can be a family, which they will see when you read the book.

I
- Pre-teach the vocabulary. Preview several pages. Have children predict what or how each picture might be a family. Use your preferred guided reading strategy to read the book.

B
- Distribute the reproducible. Count off children. Ask each child to decorate the figure and to write his or her number in the circle on it, then cut it out. Attach string or yarn to tie each figure onto coat hangers to hang overhead in the classroom. Create a class poem using the model to go with the display,

  <u>(number in your class)</u> is our family
  at school.
  Working and playing happily.

Re-source → http://www.Pammunozryan.com/hund.html
Provides activities for *One Hundred is a Family*.

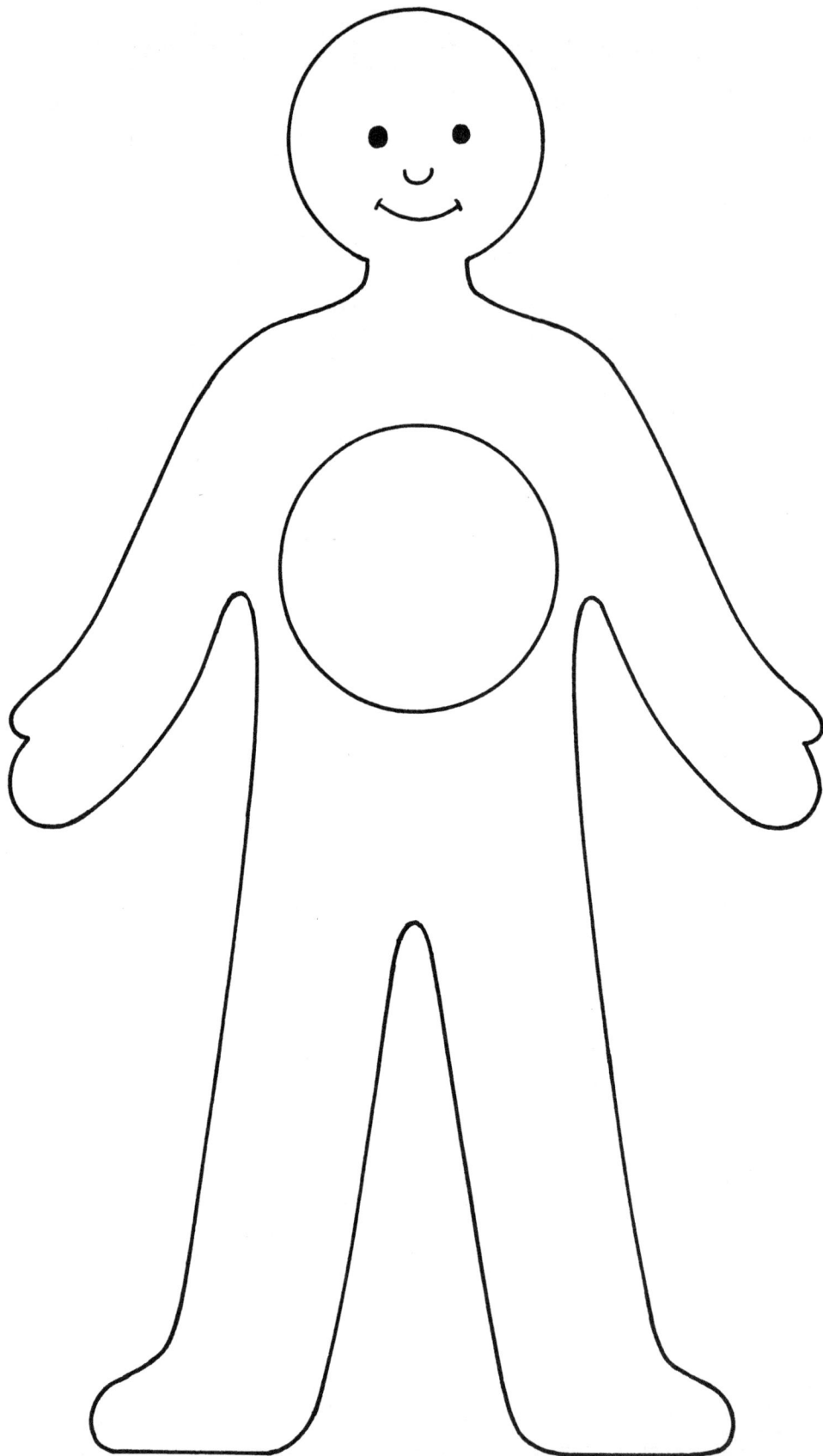

Numbers in Your Neighborhood

Key Words

up, down, high, low, words for numbers

Subjects

math, social studies, geography

Get Ready

- Scout out areas in and around your school to visit on a walking field trip designed to discover numbers in use. Choose as many areas in your neighborhood as there are groups working on this activity.
- Obtain the necessary permissions for field trips and enlist chaperones according to your district's policy.
- Writing tablets, clipboards, pencils—one per group
- Mural paper
- Art supplies (crayons, markers, glue)
- Preview the Internet site below to extend the activity.

B

- Invite the children to accompany you on a number hunt around the classroom or school to see where they can find numbers. Tell children to look up and down, high and low, even under things. After several minutes, have the children tell or point to where they saw the numbers. Suggest other places where they can find numbers that they may have overlooked (for example, on watches, serial numbers under a desk).

- Tell children that they are going to go on a number walk around their neighborhood to find numbers and tell about how they are used. Brief the groups. Give a time limit for the activity and a gathering place for all groups when they finish. Remind children to look for prices, license plates, and addresses. Have them take notes on what numbers they see. When possible, have them collect realia from the places visited, such as receipts or menus. When the students gather, have each group tell about the numbers they found.

- Review the information in a subsequent class. Invite the children to role-play what they saw people doing and how they were using numbers in their daily lives. Refer back to each group's notes. Have the children create a neighborhood number mural/collage. Encourage the children to use their realia as part of the mural/collage. Each group will contribute a section.

Re-source

http://www.mapquest.com/ or **http://www.mapblast.com**
These sites allow you to enter addresses and print maps of local neighborhoods..

How Much? How Many?

Key Words
words for articles of clothing

Subjects
math, social studies

Get Ready

- Gather clean articles of clothing. Try to find multiples so the children can practice sorting and counting. Essential items are clothes hanger, T-shirt, shirt, skirt, pants, socks, hat/cap, jacket, and gloves.
- Prepare labels/flash cards for each item of clothing (cut-outs from catalogs or Sunday newspaper inserts are good free sources of clothing pictures).
- Reproducible 17, one per child
- Preview the Internet site below to extend the activity.

B
- Show a flashcard. Help children identify the word and place it near that article of clothing. Ask one child to close his or her eyes or turn around. Rearrange the flashcards so that they are on incorrect articles of clothing. Have that child rearrange them correctly. Repeat until each child has had a turn. (Children can also do this in groups or pairs.)

I
- Use this opportunity to count, add, and subtract. Use TPR (Total Physical Response) as you give a variety of commands. For example, *Count the socks. There are 5 T-shirts. Take away 2.* Reword the everyday language into mathematical statements. For example, *5 T-shirts minus 2 T-shirts equals 3 T-shirts.* Show each equation on the board (*5 – 2 = 3*).

I
- Introduce the reproducible. Make sure the children understand each direction. Give examples, using the articles of clothing you've displayed. After children have completed the worksheet, have them talk about the mathematical operations using everyday language and the articles of clothing as props.

Re-source
http://www.walmart.com or **http://www.jcpenny.com**
Visit these catalog sites for pictures of individual items of clothing.

Name _____

1. Sum it up.

    4   +   2   = _____

2. Read the picture.

How many ▢ in all?   _____

How many have letters?   _____

How many do not?   _____

3. Take away.

    5   –   1   = _____

4. Count and think.

There are ▢▢▢▢▢▢▢ .

There are ▢▢▢▢▢▢ .

Is there one ▢ for each ▢ ?   _____

Money Counts

Key Words

money, penny, nickel, dime, quarter, half dollar, dollar

Subjects

math, social studies

Get Ready

• Real money, both paper and coins, especially lots of pennies
• Play money
• Heavy stock paper
• Adhesive tape or labels for price tags
• Preview and bookmark the Internet sites below

B • Display coins and paper money. Ask children what they recognize and name the denominations. Talk about things they can buy with it.

B • Work in groups. Have one group count coins and sort into denominations. Have others play the simple money recognition and counting games at **www.aplusmath.com/Flashcards/index.html**. Print out the pictures of currency from this site. Have children trace the shape on heavy stock paper and paste it down to make play money. Encourage them to splurge with their money making.

I • Set up a store. You might use toys, packaged food items, or school supplies. Work with children to identify what you are selling and to decide on prices. Model the language for buying and selling things as you play store. For example: *How much does this cost? This costs _____. I'd like to buy____, please. Thank you.*

Re-source

http://www.treas.gov/currency/
Learn currency fun facts and information from the U.S. Mint.

www.aplusmath.com/Flashcards/index.html

Number Game

objects, numbers 1-15

Key Words

Subjects — math

Get Ready
- Fifteen small objects that are the same (paper clips, bottle caps, etc.)
- Preview the Internet site below for more interactive games.

B
- Children work in pairs to play this simple yet challenging game. Engage children in conversation as they play. Fifteen small objects (can be candy pieces, coins, blocks, or other objects) for each pair of players are laid out to form a triangle like this:

```
        ★
      ★   ★
    ★   ★   ★
  ★   ★   ★   ★
★   ★   ★   ★   ★
```

- Children take turns removing from one to all of the objects in a horizontal row counting out loud as they do it. Whoever picks up the last object loses the game. Encourage children to play the game many times over as they would tic-tac-toe. Ask each group questions, such as *How many times did you win/lose? How did you win? What did you do first? Next? Last?*

Re-source

http://members.aol.com/_ht_a/iongoal/k2count.htm
Learn how to count with interactive games.

Key Words

Subjects

Get Ready

The Days, Months, and Year

calendar, months of the year, days of the week, before, after

math, social studies

- Photocopies of monthly calendars
- Fine line markers
- Large drawing paper (11 x 17)
- Download calendars from the Internet sites below or use other software with an available, printable monthly calendar to make this activity easier. Most programs allow you to adjust the size of the month and print one on each page. Holidays are usually included, and you may want to add special school observances (teacher conferences, and so on). Your school office may also have a master calendar to loan you. Make a copy of each month for each child.

I

- Each day hand out one month and review it as a whole class. Ask about the weather and any special holidays during that month. Have children count the days and recite the days of the week. Use the concept of *before* and *after* as well as yesterday, today, and tommorrow in your questions.

B

- Have children draw a seasonally appropriate picture above the month or a picture of something from their homelands. When all the months have been completed, staple each child's months together onto a large drawing paper (11 x 17). Children write the year in large numbers and decorate the blank spaces of the large paper.

Re-source

http://www.timeanddate.com/calendar/index.html
You can customize and print calendars from the current or a previous year. A list of holidays is also included.

http://www.englishclub.net/reference/vocabulary/wk.htm
This contains days-of-the-week charts. Go to the main page for more excellent resources for teachers.

The Seasons

Key Words
spring, summer, winter, fall (autumn)

Subjects
science

Get Ready
- Articles of clothing
- Reproducible 18, one for each child
- Preview the Internet sites below and download pictures and icons of the four seasons.

B
- Pass around pictures and icons of the four seasons. Identify the items in them. If you do not have four seasons where you live, print out a map of those places that have more dramatic seasonal changes.

I
- Display and try on various clothing articles. Review the vocabulary for articles of clothing with a guessing game. Give clues about the clothing until someone guesses correctly. For example: *I'm an article of clothing for winter. I'm worn on the feet.* Have other children take turns giving clues.

B
- Hand out the Reproducible 18. Identify the season in each picture. Have children circle the articles of clothing that are not appropriate in the picture. Engage class in a discussion of their conclusions and then have children color the pictures.

Re-source
http://www.yahooligans.com/science_and_nature/the_earth/seasons/
Contains links to information and pictures about the seasons.

http://school.discovery.com/clipart/
Discovery School's clip art gallery for seasons and holidays

Circle the clothes that are **not** correct for that season.

Spring

Summer

Fall

Winter

The Weather

Key Words

weather, forecast, temperature, cloudy, sunny, windy, rainy, snowy, foggy

Subjects

science, social studies, math

Get Ready

- Make large weather symbols (sun, clouds, rain, wind, snow) on poster board.
- Outdoor thermometer
- Map of U.S.
- Copy of reproducible weather chart below, one for each child
- Preview and bookmark the Internet site below.

B
- Hold up the weather symbols and tell children the type of weather each card represents. Practice the language. Ask: *How's the weather today?* Have children point out the correct weather symbol. Use TPR (Total Physical Response) commands such as *Show me what you do in the snow. Make a snowman.*

I
- Show children a map of the United States. Pinpoint where you live. Tell children they are going to be using the Internet to look for the weather forecast for the local area. Go to **http://www.cnn.com/WEATHER/index.html** and have someone type in the school's zip code. You will see the forecast for the next four days including the temperature highs and lows.

A
- Using the reproducible weather chart below, have children copy the five-day forecast into the Forecast boxes. Each day look at your classroom thermometer. Record daily temperatures and weather in the Actual boxes. At the end of the week, discuss the comparison between the forecast and the actual weather. Make comparisons and contrasts.

Re-source

http://www.cnn.com/WEATHER/index.html
Use this Web site to find out the weather in other states and countries.

Weather Chart

	Monday	Tuesday	Wednesday	Thursday	Friday
Forecast					
Actual					

Raindrops

Key Words

rain gauge, measure, ruler, graph, rainfall

Subjects

science, math

Get Ready

- Download instructions on how to make a rain gauge, rain gauge ruler, and graph from the Internet site below.
- Enlarge graph from the Internet site
- Straight-sided glass container
- Scissors
- Cellophane wrap
- Tape

I

- Ask children to show or tell how much rain falls in one month in the area. Tell them they are going to make a rain gauge to measure the amount of rainfall for a whole month.

B

- Follow the directions downloaded from the Web site to make a rain gauge. Use the Internet site graph to plot the amount of rainfall each day. Discuss the results at the end of each week and review at the end of the month. Have the children compare their predictions with the actual rainfall.

Re-source

http://www.miamisci.org/hurricane/rainmeasure.html
Instructions on how to make other weather instruments.

http://www.yahooligans.com/
Search "desert" and "rainforest" for pictures.

Snowy Day

Key Words

sun, rain, snow, words for kinds of storms

Subjects

language arts, social studies, science, art

Get Ready

➤ *The Snowy Day* by Ezra Jack Keats, Viking Penguin (Puffin), 1981.
● Chart paper for a weather word bank.
● Heavy poster stock or cardboard for the baseboard of the models, cut at least 3' x 3', one per group.
● Art supplies and recycled materials for making three dimensional snow models; (popcorn, plastic packing peanuts, white tissue paper, clay, twigs, aluminum foil)
● Preview and bookmark the Internet site below.

B

● Go to **http://www-geoimages.berkeley.edu/**. Choose sites that refer to your state, region, or children's home country. Randomly download the frames. (If one image does not show enough information, go quickly to the next frame.) Build a weather word bank. Ask children what kind of weather they see. Identify *sun(ny), rain, snow, kinds of storms*. List these on your word bank. (Leave space for pasting and drawing pictures around each word.) Conclude with snow pictures that will help you lead into the reading.

● Pre-teach any vocabulary. Read the book through once using your preferred guided reading strategy. On a subsequent reading go page by page, referring to the text for gestures and finger plays to accompany the reading. Like the boy in the book, walk with toes pointing in and out, dragging the feet s-l-o-w-l-y; smack a snow covered tree; make angels in the snow. Use your fingers to show snow fluttering all about.

● Have the children work in groups to make three-dimensional snowy-day play boards. Use packing peanuts and popcorn to make three-dimensional snow; crumple tissue paper for snow piles; cut out aluminum foil ice rinks. Children can use small dolls or cut out figures resembling the collage characters shown in Ezra Jack Keat's illustrations for role play or acting out parts of the book.

Re-source

http://www-geoimages.berkeley.edu/
This site is dedicated to providing geological references. Literally hundreds of pictures are available for downloading.

Snowflakes

Key Words

snow, crystals

Subjects

science, art

Get Ready

- Art supplies: construction paper, scissors, glue, glitter, tissue paper, cellophane
- Preview the Internet sites below for background and to download pictures of snow scenes and snow crystals.

- This activity is most appropriate to do when there is snow on the ground, but even if you live in a warm climate, you can investigate snow through pictures and the Internet.

I

- Show the class snow scenes. Ask: *What is snow?* Record appropriate answers on the board. Tell students that they are going to look at pictures of what makes up a snowflake.

I

- Go to **http://www.lpsi.barc.usda.gov/emusnow/**. Select magnified images to help children understand that snow crystals have different shapes. Print some of the images for the class.

B

- Allow children to decide which snow crystal shape they would like to cut out. Make the snow crystal three-dimensional, using crumpled tissue paper. Decorate with glitter and hang in the classroom.

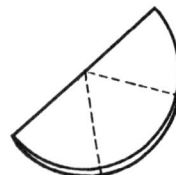

Re-source

http://www-geoimages.berkeley.edu/GeoImages/Powell/powellsnow.html
Site for snow scenes

http://www.teelfamily.com/activities/snow/
Site for background

http://www.its.caltech.edu/~atomic/snowcrystals/

Site for snow crystals

Come Again Another Day

Key Words

raining, pouring, snowing, freezing, sunny, shining

Subjects

science, music

Get Ready

- Gather pictures for the song from Internet sites, science books, periodicals, library books.
- Preview the Internet sites below for additional information.

B

- Spread the introduction of these verses over several days so that children can master one verse before introducing another. Pre-teach the new vocabulary using visuals, sound effects, and pantomime.

I

- After children are familiar with the song, divide them into three groups to come up with actions to accompany each verse. Have each group perform the song with their actions while the rest of the class helps them sing.

It's raining; it's pouring;
The old man is snoring.
Went to bed
'cause he bumped his head
And he couldn't get up in the morning.
Rain, rain, go away;
Come again another day.

It's sunny; it's shining;
The old man is dining.
Got out of bed
'cause someone said
That it looked really great in the morning.
Sun, sun don't go away;
Stay again for another day.

It's snowing; it's freezing;
The old man is sneezing.
Went to bed
'cause he bumped his head
And he couldn't get up in the morning.
Snow, snow, go away;
Come again another day.

Re-source

http://www.weather.com/
Visit this Web site for additional weather information.

http://www.yahooligans.com/science_and_nature/the-earth/weather
Links to information about the weather.

What's Big? What's Small?

Key Words

Let me tell you _____, what's, big, small

Subjects

math, science, language arts

Get Ready

- Make a transparency of the poem "Big and Small."
- Preview the Internet site below to extend the activity.

B

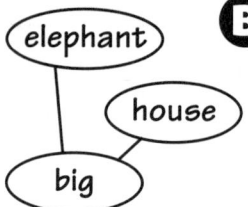

- Write the words *big* and *small* on the board. Ask the children to show you big and show you small. Brainstorm things they think are big and small. Cluster their responses in a word map. Ask them if they know other words for *big* and *small* (*large, tiny, little*). As you talk about big and small items, practice combining the adjective with the noun (Example: *tiny mouse*).

I

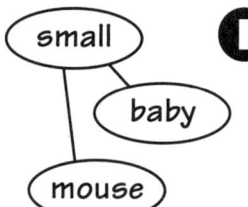

- Display the overhead transparency. Teach the poem line-by-line tracking the words. When the children know the lines, have them join in.

Word map: elephant, house, big, small, baby, mouse

Big and Small
by Christine San Jose

Let me tell you what's big.   *(Arms wide open)*
Let me tell you what's small.   *(Palms close together)*
Giraffe who stretches way up tall.   *(Arms stretched high overhead)*
A ladybug who climbs my wall.   *(Fingers moving upwards)*
Elephant loud with trumpet call.   *(Arm of child extended like a trunk)*
A squeaking mouse in the horse's stall. *(Index finger and thumb showing tiny)*
What's big? What's small?
Aren't we glad there's room for all?   *(Arms outstretched and up)*

B

- Teach the finger play. Refer the children to the word maps. Invite them to substitute other words to describe things that are big or small.

Re-source

http://www.zooweb.net/www.htm
Compare big and small by finding big and small animals.

© 2001 Rigby

Big Things, Little Things

Key Words

big, little

Subjects

math, language arts

Get Ready

- Poster paper, one sheet per group
- Art supplies (pencils, crayons)
- Preview the Internet site below to extend the activity.

B

- Use gestures to demonstrate the words *big* and *little*. Work with the children to name or point out things in the school and classroom that are big and little. List their responses under the headings *Big, Little*. Ask the children to name other things to add to the list. Additional big-little comparisons can be made by visiting **http://www.zooweb.net/www.htm** and comparing animal sizes.

I

- Have the children work in small groups. Have each group work together to fill up their poster paper with words and pictures of things that are either big or little. Tell half of the groups to find big things and half of the groups to find small things. Invite them to share their posters with the class as part of a guessing game. Have volunteers describe one item with words and pantomime, but without naming it. Ask the others in the class to guess what it is.

B

- When possible, use their drawings to illustrate what things go from little to big. (For example, a seed grows into a plant, a baby grows up to become an adult, one piece of trash after another becomes a garbage dump, and one piece of sand after another becomes a beach. Or show a long pencil and one that has been sharpened almost down to the eraser.) Have the children act out each of these things going from little to big, crouching down small or stretching up tall.

Re-source

http://www.zooweb.net/www.htm
Compare big and small by finding large and small animals.

Shapes in Space

Key Words — rectangle, triangle, circle, semicircle, square, hop, rock, tap, tip, tilt, step, stop, stack, take, watch, toss, dance

Subjects — math, language arts, physical education

Get Ready — ◤*Shape Space* by Cathryn Falwell, Houghton Mifflin (Clarion), 1992.
- Cover a box with colored paper.
- Use colored construction paper, newsprint, and magazines for paper stock. Cut out enough geometric shapes so each child can receive 2-3 shapes (see the key words).
- Poster paper
- Reproducible 19, one for each child
- Preview the Internet site below for additional resources.

B

- Invite each child to pick two or three shapes out of the box without looking. Help the children identify the shapes. Have them work in small groups or with partners as they create one or more things from their shapes (a building, a face, a creature, or an animal). Have them go from group to group as they look at and talk about what each group made.

- Introduce the book by previewing the pages. Point out any shapes in the book that are similar to what the children made. Read the book through once using your preferred guided reading strategy. Use TPR (Total Physical Response) to have children learn and practice the verbs, such as *hop, tap dance.*

- Distribute the reproducible. Explain to children that they should draw a picture or write the word for any object they see around them that has the shape listed at the head of each column. Start in the classroom, go around the school, and go outdoors to find things. When you regroup, make poster word banks with words and pictures for each shape. Use the posters to generate language and as prompts for talking about what the children see around them.

Re-source — **http://www.forum.swarthmore.edu/math.topics.html**
Visit this site or search others under the subject "geometry" to find interesting representations of shapes.

▭ Rectangle	△ Triangle	◯ Circle	⌒ Semicircle	▢ Square

Shape Game

Key Words

oval, triangle, pentagon, hexagon, star, square, rectangle, semicircle, circle

Subjects

math, physical education

Get Ready

- A bean bag
- 1 paper plate
- Tag board to make small arrow for spinner
- 1 brass fastener
- Shapes cut from file folders or construction paper
- Preview the Internet site below for additional information.

B

- Make a large grid on the floor with masking tape with three boxes across and three boxes down. Place a different shape in each box. Make a spinner using a paper plate, a tag board arrow, and the fastener. Draw each shape around the spinner. If your class or group is large, make two grids, shapes, and spinners.

- Be the first person to spin. Choose a volunteer to be the tosser. Spin the arrow on the plate and tell the shape to the tosser. The tosser throws the bean bag to the box containing that shape. If the child tosses correctly, he or she will become the spinner for the next volunteer. If the toss is not correct, or doesn't land on the correct square, that child sits down and another child takes a turn on the next spin. The spinner stays on the job until the tosser wins and moves on to become spinner.

- Keep the grid on the floor for some weeks so that small groups can play during free time.

- *Variation:* The spinner will spin and give the command, "Put your right foot on the _____." Then spin for the left foot location, right hand, and left hand. The child is a winner if s/he can put both feet and hands in the correct places without falling.

Re-source

http://www.forum.swarthmore.edu/math.topics/html
Visit this site or search others under the subject "geometry" to find interesting representations of shapes.

Shapes in Color

Key Words

circle, triangle, square, rectangle, fold, dip, squeeze

Subjects

art, math

Get Ready

- Bottles of food coloring, muffin tins, white tissue paper, lots of newspaper, water
- Cover tables with newspaper. Fill the cups of the muffin tins: some with water and some with food coloring. Place a muffin tin in the middle of each table.
- Parent or other adult volunteers
- Preview the Internet site below for extending the activity.

1

- Model for children how to fold a sheet of white tissue paper in many different ways (as triangles, squares, and so on) until the tissue paper is a 4" folded shape. Have each child fold 3 or 4 individual sheets of tissue paper.

- Take one folded shape and dip a corner into the plain water first (it is very important to dip it in water first) and then into one of the cups of colored water. Repeat with another corner and another color (always dipping the paper in the plain water first) until all the corners have been colored.

- Put the shape between several sheets of folded newspaper on the floor and step on the shape to squeeze out the excess water. Put full weight on your step to squeeze really well. Repeat this several times, each time moving the shape to a different section of the newspaper.

- Gently and carefully unfold the shape to its original size and observe the colorful tie-dyed designs on the paper. Drape the paper over a chair for a few minutes so it can dry completely.

- When all have finished the tie-dying process, have children look over the results and identify the shapes they see on the paper. No two tie-dyed papers will be the same. These papers can be used for wrapping paper, covering wastebaskets and boxes, wall hangings, or for background on a bulletin board or wall.

Re-source

http://www.yahooligans.com/arts_and_entertainment/art/activities/
Provides links to art information and activities.

Alike and Different

Key Words

pattern, nature, symmetry, alike, different

Subjects

science, math

Get Ready

- Collect things that show patterns such as pieces of material, wrapping paper, pictures of abstract paintings.
- Drawing paper
- Magazines
- Art supplies (crayons and markers)
- Preview the Internet sites below to extend the activity.

- Display pattern samples. Point out the patterns. Count repeating colors and items. Tell children these are called patterns—units or groups of units that repeat.

- Discuss the terms *alike* and *different*. Revisit the pattern samples. Have children point out designs and patterns that are alike and different. Then have children search through magazines for examples of patterns in food, living things, and plants. Each child should choose at least one pattern that they want to share with the class. Talk about the color, shape, and size. Turn the pictures into a class collage.

- Use the Internet sites below to show patterns that are symmetrical.

Re-source

http://www.scienceU.com/geometry/
This site shows symmetry on tile designs.

http://www.smm.org/sln/tf/s/symmetry/symmetry.html
Use this site to show symmetrical patterns of butterflies.

Measuring All Around You

Key Words

miles, measurement, map

Subjects

math, social studies, physical education

Get Ready

- Find a large map of your county to hang in your classroom.
- Go to the Internet site below to find a map of your county. Print and photocopy one for each child.

1

- Show that small steps, bit by bit, translate into many miles. Get daily, virtual exercise by "walking" across your county without ever leaving the school. This can be started at any time during the year. Write on the board: *1 mile = 5,280 feet.* Measure a "track" space around the outer edge of the classroom or up and down the hall. Calculate how much of a mile it is equal to. Then calculate how many times you will have to go around to equal one mile.

- During recess or other free time in the class, have children start walking and measuring out the miles, little by little. Plot the progress on your large classroom map. Add up the number of feet and subtract from 5,280. Plot it on the map. Use various sites or towns as landmarks, saying, "We have arrived in _____ today!" Have children mark the progress on their small versions of the map.

Re-source

http://www.census.gov/cgi-bin/gazetteer/
Locate a map of your county on this site.

http://www.mapquest.com or www.mapblast.com
Plot the distance and route between addresses. Point out places children should know (police, hospital, home, and school).

Measuring the Statue of Liberty

Key Words

Statue of Liberty, immigrant, inch, foot, yard, ruler, yardstick, tape measure

Subjects

math, social studies, history

Get Ready

- A ruler, a yardstick, and tape measure
- A ball of string and scissors
- Masking tape and marker
- Preview and bookmark the Internet site below.

1

- Go on a virtual tour of the Statue of Liberty on **http://www.nyctourist.com/liberty1.htm.** While the children focus on the pictures, act as their guide by paraphrasing the text. Point out that the Statue of Liberty stands in New York Harbor. The Statue of Liberty was a gift from France, and we think of it as a symbol welcoming new people–immigrants–to the United States.

- Introduce or review the instruments of measurement by having the children identify them. Have children use them to measure various objects and tell their measurement in inches, feet, or yards.

- Write the following measurements for the Statue of Liberty on the board.

head	17 feet wide	nose	$4\frac{1}{2}$ feet long
face	10 feet wide	finger	8 feet long
mouth	1 yard wide		

   Have the children work in small groups to measure and cut each of the above lengths from the ball of string. Use the masking tape to make labels. Label each string by body part and length.

- Have each group use their measuring strings to compare the measurements of the Statue of Liberty with things in the classroom or on the playground. When the groups come together, have them talk about what they found. Encourage the children to make simple equations and comparisons. For example: *The mouth equals two desks. The head of the Statue is longer than the blackboard.*

Re-source

http://www.nyctourist.com/liberty1.htm

Your Weight in Other Worlds

Key Words — light, heavy, pounds, ounces, names for the planets and stars

Subjects — science, math

Get Ready
- A variety of light and heavy items for weighing and containers that show weight (canned and packaged goods)
- A kitchen or laboratory scale and bathroom scale
- Index cards
- Preview and bookmark the Internet site below.

1
- Display the items. Have the children identify what they can. Pass the items around. Point out how the children can find the weight of each item. Weigh other items on display, using the different scales. List items and their weights on the chalkboard. Weigh each child and write their weight on an index card. Help children compare how much they weigh to the items displayed. (Examples: *Do you weigh more than the jar of peanut butter? Do you weigh less?*)

- Invite children to go with you on a trip through space. Explain that things do not weigh what they do here on earth. Have volunteers act out and tell about how they might get to space and explore the planets and stars. Go to: **http://www.exploratorium.edu/ronh/weight**. Scroll through the screen to identify the planets. Click on any of the planets for more detailed information and pictures. Shelter and paraphrase the text.

- Have the children calculate how much they weigh in space at the same site. Have each child enter his or her weight in the box on the screen in order to calculate how much they weigh on other planets. Have the children select favorite planets. Have them scroll to that planet to see and tell how much they weigh. (Example: *On the moon, I weigh twenty pounds*). Compare and contrast how much things weigh on earth and on other planets. Revisit the items the children have displayed and weighed. Have them compare their weights to the displayed items. (Example: *I weigh twenty pounds. Twenty pounds equals twenty bags of sugar.*)

Re-source — **http://www.exploratorium.edu/ronh/weight**

On a Ride to Yesterday

Key Words

yesterday, history words, look, see

Subjects

history, social studies, language arts

Get Ready

- Individual school pictures or a photocopy of a head shot of each child
- 5" x 7" index cards, at least one per student
- Use a quarter to trace circles on construction paper to use as wheels, two per child.
- Set up four or five history stations in the classroom (Examples: the dinosaurs; castles and knights, pioneers and cowboys, early twentieth century). Display covers from storybooks, pages from history books, and online pictures. At each station, have a piece of chart paper to create a word bank.
- Art supplies (paste, markers, crayons)
- Download and print photos or clip art from Internet sources like **http://www.yahooligans.com/downloader/pictures/school_bell/Social_studies/history/**.

B

- Have children line up and link their left arm to the shoulder of the child in front, making a pretend train. Make train sounds and motions as you move about the room. Ask the children to point out things they see outside the window. Encourage conversation. For example: tell them to *Look!* or *See the _____ .* Ask: *What do you see?*)

- Tell the children they're going on a ride to yesterday. Move from station to station. Have the children identify things that they see in the pictures. List these on chart paper at each station. (With small groups, invite children on a virtual museum tour by searching for the Web site of a local museum.)

- Distribute an index card and two wheels to each child. Have children paste their pictures on index cards as if they were looking out a window. Have them add the wheels and draw a picture on the card of something from their trip to yesterday. Help them write down the name of the thing they drew. Display the cards on a wall or bulletin board. Use the train as a prompt for individual or class storytelling or for role-plays in small groups.

Re-source

http://www.yahooligans.com/downloader/pictures/school_bell/Social_studies/history/
This site provides a resource for historical pictures. You may also want to search for a local history museum's Web site.

http://www.americanhistory.si.edu
A Smithsonian Institution site

http://www.ucmp.berkeley.edu/subway/
A University of California site

Long Long Ago: The Dinosaurs

Key Words

dinosaur, short, long, big, tall, neck, teeth

Subjects

history, science, language arts

Get Ready

• Preview and bookmark the Internet sites below.
Go to **www.childrensmuseum.org**. Select <u>Fun on-line</u>. Click on the dinosaur icon or <u>Kinetosaurs</u> on the tool bar. Select <u>Dinosaur Database</u>. Click on the name of a dinosaur. Scroll down below the color picture to click on text for a blackline master to print and reproduce, at least one per child.

1

• Ask children to use their imaginations to go back in time, long, long ago. Ask them what animals would they see? Accept all responses. Remind them that they would see the dinosaurs. Go to **www.childrensmuseum.org/dino.htm** Take a look at the T-Rex mascot outside the museum. Go to <u>Dinosaur Database</u>. Select from the dinosaurs listed. Paraphrase the information and shelter the English. Point out characteristics. (For example: long neck, short legs, sharp teeth).

• Distribute blackline dinosaurs. Have children learn the names and color the pictures. Work with children to write or dictate a sentence about it.

• Go to **www.rain.org/~philfear/download-a-dinosaur.html**. Invite children to see if their dinosaur is on the list of cutouts. Download the dinosaur cutouts and instructions. Guide children to put together the dinosaur as you generate descriptive words about them. (Example: Triceratops has three horns. This dinosaur has a long neck.) Use the dinosaur cutouts and coloring pages to create a display. Add ferns (real or made from construction or crepe paper), caves made from clay, rocks, sand, and dirt.

Re-source

www.childrensmuseum.org
The Children's Museum of Indianapolis has more fun things to do with dinosaurs.

www.rain.org/~philfear/download-a-dinosaur.html

Long Ago: Native American Rock Art

Key Words

art, Native Americans

Subjects

social studies, art

Get Ready

- Cut brown paper bags into approx. 7" x 10" pieces, one per child
- Art supplies (charcoal or colored chalk)
- Preview and bookmark the Internet site below.

I

- Go to **net.indra.com/~dheyser/rockart.html**. Select examples of rock art from the gallery. Tell children these are examples of rock art made by Native Americans perhaps thousands of years ago. Explore with children what they think the pictures look like. Explain that we are not sure of their meaning. They may tell stories. Print out the rock art that you've discussed.

B

- Distribute the art supplies. Have children draw their favorite symbol onto a piece of brown paper bag using colored chalk.

A

- Choose one or more examples of rock art from the Internet. Model as you work with children to tell a story about one of the pictures. Then have the children work in small groups to create a story. Have children share their story with the class, revise it, and practice telling it. You may wish to tape record the final versions of their stories and display the rock art to share with other classes and family members.

Re-source

net.indra.com/~dheyser/rockart.html
Southwest U.S. Rock Art Gallery

Yesterday, Today, Tomorrow

Key Words

yesterday, today, tomorrow, Monday, Tuesday, Wednesday, Thursday, Friday, Saturday, Sunday, before, after

Subjects

math, social studies

Get Ready

- Small and large white paper plates, one per child
- Metal fasteners, one per child
- Reproducible 20 (word cards), one per child
- Art supplies (rulers, scissors, glue, markers)
- Make a large circle on the chalk board divided into 7 sections
- Preview the Internet site below for additional resources.

1

- Ask volunteers to name the days of the week. Hand out small paper plates. Tell children they will work on the back side of each plate. Help children use the ruler to divide the small plate into seven equal sections. (Tip: Buy plates with ridges around the outside. Count the total number of ridges and divide by 7 to make equal sections.) Have children cut out the days of the week word cards. Help them identify the words and line them up in order. Have them paste each word to the outermost portion of each section. Set the small paper plate on top of the large one. Help children make a hole through the middle of both and fasten with a metal fastener. Then have them extend the lines from the small plate to the end of the large one. (See page 94.)

- Draw on the board a large circle around the smaller one. Ask a volunteer to name today's day. Write *today* above it. In the sections to the left and right of *today*, write *yesterday* and *tomorrow*. Have children point to the name of today's day on their plate wheel. Ask them to write *today* above it on the large plate and *yesterday* to the left and *tomorrow* to the right as you have modeled.

- Model practice dialogues. (Example: *What is today? Today is Monday. Tomorrow is Tuesday.*) Have children practice with a partner. Monitor children's comprehension.

Re-source

http://www.englishclub.net/reference/vocabulary/wk.htm
This contains days-of-the-week charts. Go to the main page for more excellent resources for teachers.

Monday

Tuesday

Wednesday

Thursday

Friday

Saturday

Sunday

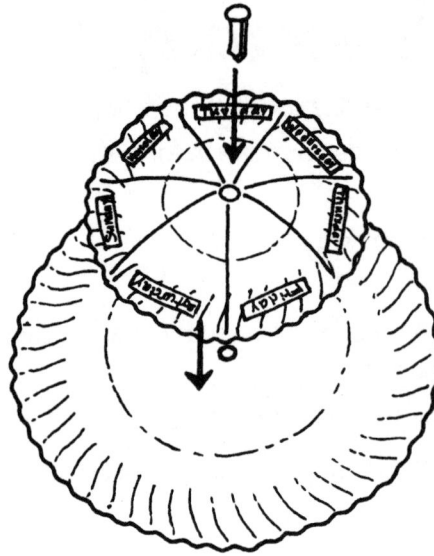

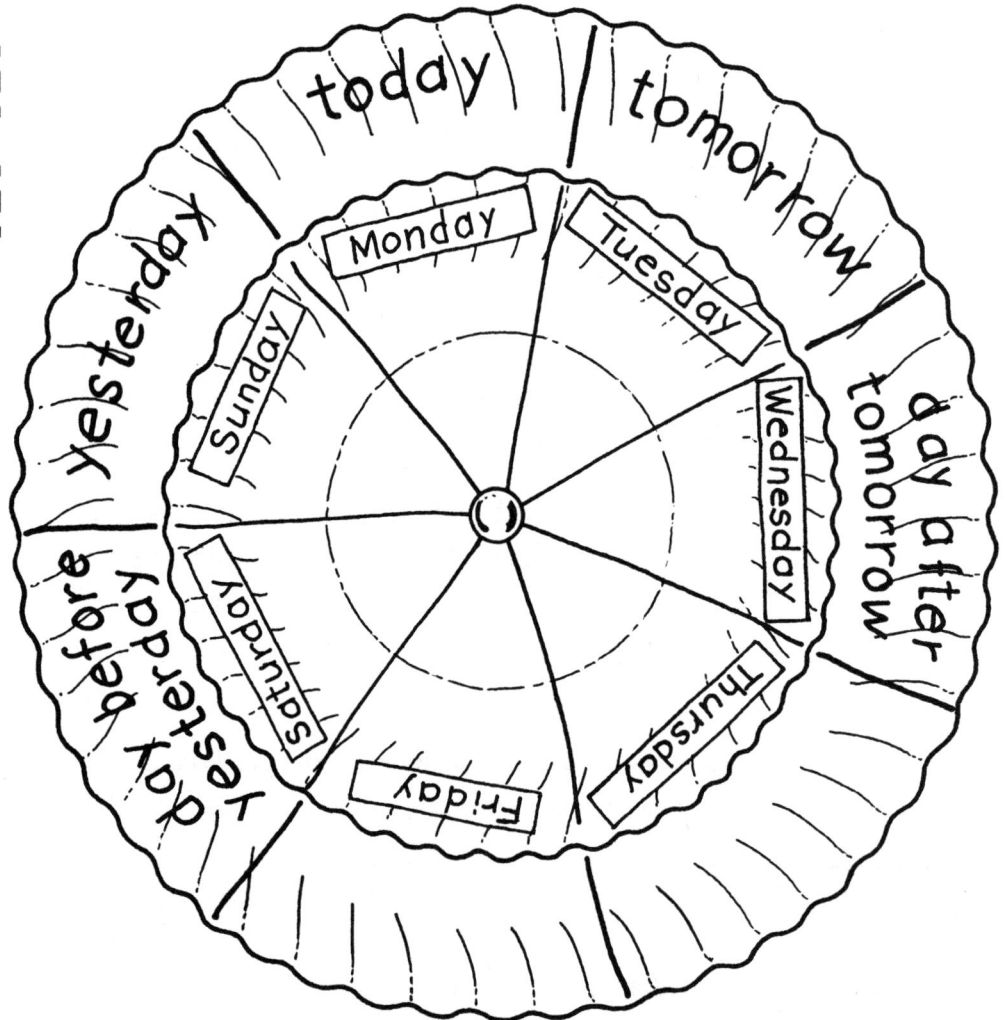

People Who Knew Yesterday

Key Words

memory, shells, puppet, medal, football

Subjects

language arts, social studies

Get Ready

📖 *Wilfred Gordon McDonald Partridge* written by Mem Fox, illustrated by Julie Vivas, Kane/Miller, 1995. (Available on audiocassette)

- Make a set of word/picture cards, Reproducible 21, one for each child.
- Bring in photographs of elderly people you know and love. Ask the children to bring in their own photographs of grandparents or other elderly relatives and friends.
- Gather supplies for making memory baskets: boxes, baskets, or bags; cutouts, stickers, art supplies.
- Preview the Internet site below for background.

I

- To prepare the children for this story, name and talk about grandparents and older people you know, who they are, where they live, what they do. Encourage the children to talk about older people in their lives and explore their notions of what "old" means. Share photographs.

A

- Ask the children to identify the words on the picture cards. Preview the pictures in the story. As you do, tell the children to hold up a picture card when they see it illustrated. Tell the children that this is a story about someone who lost her memory. Ask children to think about a time when they lost something and how it made them feel. Brainstorm the word *memory* with the children; map the responses on chart paper. Read and reread the story using your preferred guided reading strategy. As the children acquire more language, add new words and ideas to your map.

I

- Work in groups or as a class to create and decorate your own memory baskets. Each child should contribute something from home or school that reminds him or her of some person, place, or activity. (It might be a postcard, a souvenir, a ticket stub–something that does not have real value.) From time to time refer to the memory basket and have a child select a memento and tell the story behind it.

Re-source

http://www.memfox.net

This site provides background on author Mem Fox and her books, including *Wilfred Gordon McDonald Partridge*.

shell

puppet

medal

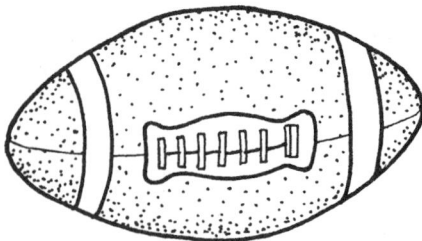

football

Our Senior Friends

Key Words

senior citizen, friend, words of introduction

Subjects

history, social studies, language arts

Get Ready

- Invite senior citizens to your classroom. (Retired teachers often enjoy coming back to help out.) Prepare them to talk about and to show photographs of times when they were growing up. You may also arrange a visit to a community senior center.
- A time line calibrated in increments starting at the birthday of the senior citizen and ending in the present.

A

- Before you visit with your guest, help the children understand the timeframe by having them tell you about people and things that they think are old. Establish dates and mark them on your time line. Tell them about your visitor. Point out on the time line the birthday of your visitor and the distance between that and your end date. Brainstorm questions that they would like to ask your guest about when they were young. Write those questions on the board. Role-play introductions and practice asking the questions.

- Inform your guest of the structure and questions that will follow. Introduce your guest and continue with discussion, questions, and answers. Follow-up with a thank-you card or email.

- Tell children that the class can adopt one or more senior friends. Compose an introductory email. Go to **http://www.indiana.edu/~eric_rec/seniors/spie.html**. The class can then select carefully-screened seniors who are ready to answer their questions and begin friendly correspondence. **Caution:** *This activity is to be done with teacher direction, according to district policy. Monitor what information is sent and received.*

Re-source

http://www.indiana.edu/~eric_rec/seniors/spie.html

Me Yesterday and Me Today

Key Words

history, time line, event, birthday, first, next, last

Subjects

history, social studies, art

Get Ready

- $8\frac{1}{2}$" x 11" drawing paper, one per child
- Art supplies (crayons, markers, scissors, and glue)
- Strips from butcher paper cut to 6" x 24", one per student
- Preview and bookmark the Internet site below.

- Explain that a time line is a series of events listed in the order that they happened. Show examples of time lines printed out from the Internet. Tell children that they are going to make time lines of their lives. Ask children to close their eyes and think about two important things in their lives. Suggest these might include a birthday party, their first day at school, or coming to the U.S. Remind them that it must have happened long ago. Have children share the events by telling or acting them out. List their responses.

- Distribute drawing paper to the children. Guide them as they fold it into quarters and then number each section 1, 2, 3, 4. Have them draw something depicting their day of birth for number 1 and an event that happened recently for number 4. Review the list and have them draw in two other important events. Have children talk about their drawings and label the events.

- Have children take the drawings home along with a letter to family members. Ask the family members to provide the dates for the events that the children listed. After the children bring the drawings back to school, have them cut out each picture. Have children sequence the events. Discuss what happened first, next, and last. Mount the pictures in order on the strip of butcher paper. Connect the pictures with a line to make the time line. Label it "My Time Line." Refer to the time line to tell personal histories. Model the language. (Example: *When I was* *years old, I _____* or *In 19__, I _____*).

Re-source

http://www.yahooligans.com/school_bell/social_studies/history/timelines/
Select time lines from the index that will be of interest to your students (from the history of bubble gum to the history of Mexico).

We See the Moon

Key Words

I see ____ ; sun, sea, river, mountains, tree, birds, flowers, bee, lake, star, house, moon

Subjects

language arts, science

Get Ready

📖 *I See The Moon and the Moon Sees Me* by Jonathan London, illustrated by Peter Fiore, Viking Penguin (Puffin), 1998.
- Place the poetry starter found below at the bottom of an $8\frac{1}{2}$" x 11" sheet of paper. Make a copy for each child.
- Art supplies (scissors, glue, markers, crayons)
- Preview and bookmark the Internet sites listed below.

B
- Engage children in a call and response format, using the sentence frame:

  I see (Pedro), and (Pedro) sees me.

- Encourage them to respond, using your name then the names of other children. Invite them to look outdoors and use the same sentence frame for things you see in your surroundings. (*I see the (sky), and the (sky) sees me.*)

B
- Preview the title and cover of the book. Show one or two examples in the book. Read the book, using your preferred guided reading strategy. Encourage the children to identify what they see in the pictures and to join in with the repetitive verses.

I
- To prepare children for writing their own poems, go to **Yahooligans**. «Search» Pictures: Moon or go to: **http://www.fys.ruu.nl/~zagers/maan/eng/maan.html**. Have the children act out exploring the moon through pretend telescopes or by walking on it. Help them identify the pictures. Tell children they are going to make books like the one they read. Distribute the poetry frame below. Revisit examples from the book. Have the children illustrate their poems. Make a class book of their poems.

> I see the _____,
> and the _____ sees me.
> Hello, _____.
> _____.

Re-source

http://www.fys.ruu.nl/~zagers/maan/eng/maan.html

http://www.yahooligans.com/downloader/pictures/
Go to this page and choose space from the menu, then solar system, then moon.

© 2001 Rigby

101 Activities for English Language Learning **99**

We Observe the Sun

Key Words

sun, shadow, times of day, longest, shortest

Subjects

science, math, language arts

Get Ready

- Make shadow boards for each group of students. Use a small mound of clay to stick a pencil or craft stick onto a piece of thick-ply cardboard as shown, one per group.
- This is a sunny day activity.
- With yellow chalk draw a large sun with rays on the board.
- A wind-up clock
- Rulers
- Reproducible 22, one per student
- Preview the Internet site below for background.

- Use the sun drawn on the board as a semantic map. Write the word *sun* in the middle. Brainstorm as many words as possible related to the sun. Ask questions. For example: *What does the sun do? How does it help us? What does it look like?* Map children's responses on each of the rays. Remind children that the sun also makes shadows. Demonstrate by shining a flashlight at the pencil on the shadow board.

- Work outside with the children. Give each group a shadow board. Draw a long line on the playground. (You'll need to designate your observation area as a no-play zone for the day.) Tell children to place their shadow boards on the line. Mark each group's place on the line. Tell children that they will keep their shadow boards in the same place all day. Have children observe the shadow on their boards. Tell them to mark the top of the shadow with a dot. Record each time of day. Tell children to write the time next to the dot. Do this three or four times throughout the day.

- On the next day, have children regroup. Have them link each dot to the mound of clay. Measure the length of each shadow. Record the time in sequence and the length of the shadow on the chart. Have children name the times of day and the length of the shadow. Talk about the longest shadow and the shortest shadow.

Re-source

http://seds.lpl.arizona.edu/nineplanets/nineplantes/sol.html
This site provides information on and images of the sun and the nine planets.

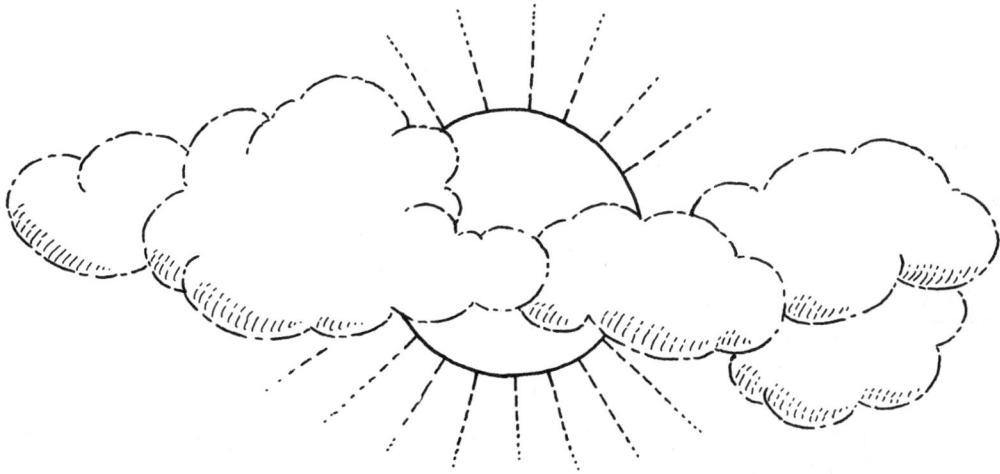

Time	Length of Shadow

We Look at the Clouds

Key Words — clouds, cumulonimbus, cirrus, cumulus, stratus, low, high

Subjects — language arts, science, technology

Get Ready
- Plastic bottles
- Ice cubes
- Cotton
- Art supplies (drawing paper, crayons or markers, paste)
- Preview and bookmark the Internet sites below to show children.

B • Take children outdoors, look out the window, or show pictures of a sky with clouds. Ask them what they see. Introduce the word *cloud*. Invite children to draw the shapes of clouds on the board.

A • Gather children around the computer. Model selecting and showing the Web sites you've bookmarked. Then have children work in pairs or groups to view the sites. Print pictures that show the four basic types of clouds: **Cumulonimbus, Cirrus, Cumulus, Stratus**. Label the pictures and discuss. For example, compare and contrast the color and shape of the clouds. Have children show you a high cloud and a low cloud. Ask: *What is a cloud? What do you think it is made of?* List responses.

B • Have children work in pairs or small groups to form each one of the four types of clouds, using the cotton and art supplies. Have them label each type. Introduce or review such adjectives as *large, small, big, little, high, low*.

I • *Optional:* Show children how to make a cloud. Fill a clear plastic bottle (small neck) with very hot water and let it sit for 3-4 minutes. Then pour out most of the water, leaving about 2 centimeters at the bottom. Fill a control bottle with the same amount (2 centimeters) of cold water. Then place an ice cube in each bottle. Have volunteers do the same. Observe, point out, and discuss how a foggy cloud forms in the bottle with hot water. Draw a digram of what happens.

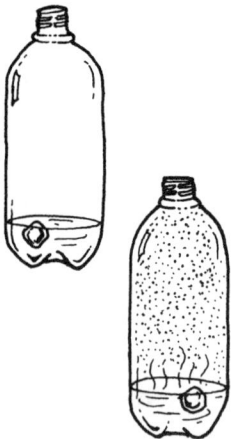

Re-source
http://vortex.plymouth.edu/clouds.html
Plymouth State College Meteorology Program provides a cloud boutique.

We Dance with the Stars

Key Words

author, poem, star, danced, born

Subjects

science, language arts

Get Ready

- Hang white twinkling holiday lights overhead.
- Make an overhead transparency of the poem printed below.
- Art supplies (drawing paper, star stickers, crayons, markers)
- Preview the Internet site below for additional information.

B

- You may wish to introduce the poem by telling them the author, the person who wrote this poem, is the most famous poet in the English language (Shakespeare). Teach the words of the poem by reading it once as you track the words on the overhead.

> A star danced   *(point overhead and dance in place)*
> and under that
> was I born.   *(cradle a baby)*

- Invite the children to join in and repeat it until they are comfortable with the words. Add gestures and as a group improvise a star dance.

I

- Brainstorm other words for *danced*. Invite children to act out other actions. Suggest things that children play outdoors (*ran, skipped, hopped, jumped*).

I

- Write the poetry frame on the board.

> A star _____
> and under that
> _____ was born.

- Have the children copy it and substitute a word for *danced* and their own name.

- Have the children decorate their poems with stars, moons, and suns. Attach string and hang these overhead.

- *Optional:* Substitute a word for *star*.

Re-source

http://www.ulen.com/Shakespeare/
Surf this site for information and background on Shakespeare and his works.

We Explore Our Planet

Key Words

forest, rainforest, desert, mountains, farm

Subjects

social studies, geography, science

Get Ready

- Heavy stock drawing paper, one per child
- Art supplies (craft sticks, crayons, markers, razor knife or scissors)
- Preview the Internet site below to select pictures for a bulletin board display.

1

- Look at the bulletin board display or the Internet pictures. Prompt children with questions such as *Who lives there? What do they do? What do they wear? What is the weather like?* Create a word web for each environment (forest, rainforest, desert, mountains, farm).

- Invite the children to choose a favorite environment—one that is different from their own. Tell them to fill up the page with a drawing of that place, using the Internet pictures for ideas. (These drawings become a backdrop.) Have them draw a face at the top of the craft stick, telling them they can be either a person or animal visiting that place. Cut a long, horizontal slit about two inches up from the bottom of the page that begins and ends about an inch from the right and left side. Show them how to insert their stick puppet in this slit and move it around.

- Work with volunteers to create a story about their environment as told by their stick puppet moving from place to place. Refer to the word webs to generate language. Then have children work with partners to role-play asking and answering questions and telling stories about visiting their environment.

Re-source

http://www.yahooligans.com/downloader/pictures/
Search Pictures forest; Pictures rain forest, Pictures desert; Pictures mountains, Pictures farm. Create a bulletin board display with the pictures and labels. Print out your favorite photos or clip art from the variety of sites. For small group work, select the sites you will end up with, but do each search word separately, encouraging children to type in the words.

We Give to the Earth

Key Words

gift, earth, air, water, soil, fire, food

Subjects

language arts, art, social studies, science

Get Ready

- A colorfully wrapped gift box with representative pictures of animals, plants, and inanimate objects from nature.
- Large sheets of newsprint or butcher paper
- Reproducible 23 for making a block, one per child
- Preview the Internet sites below for background and pictures.

A
- Show children a gift box and ask them what it is and what could be inside it. Talk about gifts and why we give or receive them. Open the box with a good deal of fanfare and show the pictures inside. Tell the children that Native Americans felt that they received gifts from Mother Earth. Ask how could these pictures be gifts or presents? Encourage children to name other "gifts" that come from nature or the earth. Are these things important to us? Why? What if they did not exist?

I
- Use large sheets of newsprint to categorize the children's ideas about what gifts we receive from the earth. Use categories such as animals, plants, food, and natural resources. (There may be some overlap in ideas.)

I
- Children cut out the block pattern and make their Gifts of the Earth block by illustrating or finding pictures of six of the words from the list, one for each part of the block. Help them fold and glue it into a block shape. This becomes their Block of Gifts. In small groups children pass around their blocks, helping to tell in which categories each gift belongs.

Re-source

http://www.germantown.k12.il.us/html/culture.html
This site provides background on Native American cultures.

http://www.yahooligans.com/downloader/pictures/
This site provides pictures for the activity.

Cut on the dotted lines and fold on the solid lines.

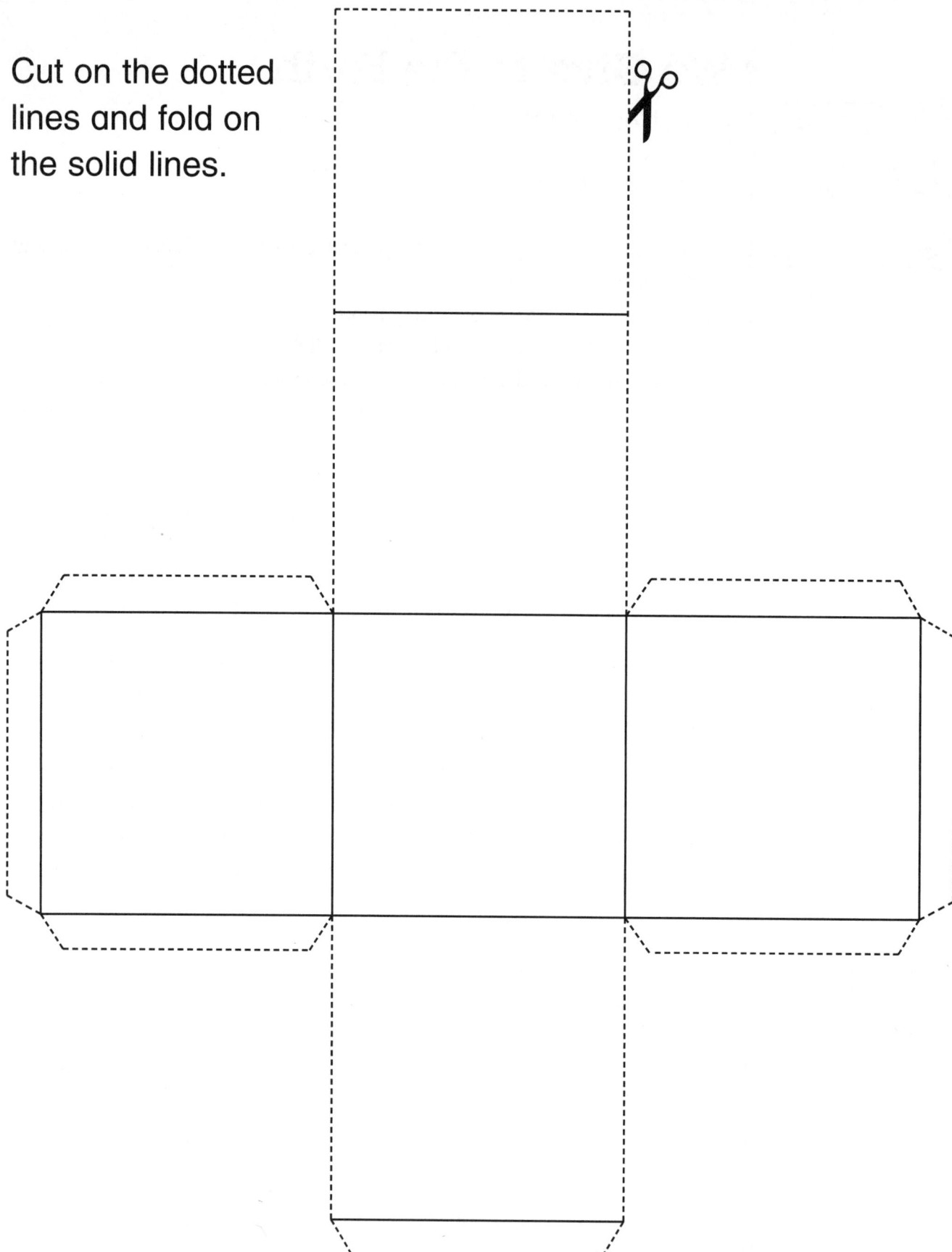

We Visit Outer Space

Key Words

alien, space, legs, arms, bodies, heads

Subjects

science, language arts

Get Ready

- Tag board
- Art supplies (crayons, markers, scissors, paste, glue, craft sticks)
- Preview and download pictures from the Internet site below.

I • Discuss the proper definition of alien as a person or creature who is not a native of a location. Dispel any negative connotations or associations with the word.

B • Go for a ride in a spaceship and walk in space. Choose a planet or destination. Have the children follow you as you walk around the classroom looking at pictures that you've downloaded and posted. Wave hello to the space creatures. Practice conversations. Give TPR (Total Physical Response) commands. (For example: *Let's float up high, down low. Walk with big steps. Go to the right/left. Wave hello.*)

• Show the blackline alien parts that you've downloaded. Help children name each body part. Tell the children to select a body, arms, and legs and put them together. Have them color and cut out their space creature. Help them paste them down and mount it on tag board. Secure craft sticks to the back to make them into puppets.

• Use the creatures for practice dialogues and role-play. Practice survival language, greetings, giving directions, describing things, and making friends.

Re-source

www.alienexplorer.com

This is a fun, child-oriented site. Select <u>Free Clip Art</u>. Download aliens, spaceships, planets, moons, and asteroids. Post around the classroom. Select <u>Create an Alien</u>. Download <u>heads</u>, <u>bodies</u>, and <u>legs</u>. Print out, reproduce, and cut apart each blackline so children can make their own space creatures.

UNIT 10: GROWING THINGS

Seeds

Key Words
seed, tiny, big(ger), small(er), large(r), tall(er), autumn, winter, spring, summer

Subjects
science, language arts, math

Get Ready

▰ *The Tiny Seed* by Eric Carle, Simon and Schuster, 1987.
- Display in order realia for growing things: a seed, a pot of dirt, small shovel, and a large plant. (If possible, provide seedlings or the plant in an earlier stage of growth.)
- Index cards or heavy stock $8\frac{1}{2}$"x 11" drawing paper cut into four pieces, 8 to 16 small cards per child
- Preview the Internet site below to extend this activity.

B
- Pre-teach the life cycle of a plant using the realia. After you have the children identify the items for growing plants, give each child a seed. Encourage children to go through the actions of planting the seed and then growing up to be the tall plant. As you do, make comparisons (*The seed is tiny. The plant is growing larger. It is tall.*) Draw a diagram of the process in 1, 2, 3 order.

B
- Preview several pictures in the book. As you do, point out the sequence that carries the seed to plant. Pre-teach the necessary vocabulary. Use your preferred guided reading strategy to read the book.

I
- Have the children make a flip-book of a seed growing. Refer children to the story for ideas. Explain that each picture will show the plant growing bigger or taller, but only so slightly. Emphasize and monitor that the children are drawing each picture in the same spot on each page. Have the children make covers for their books and lay out the drawings in order. Have them staple the books together. Children can watch the plant "grow" as they flip the book.

Re-source
http://www.urbanext.uiuc.edu/gpe/
The Great Plant Escape activity teaches about seeds and plants.

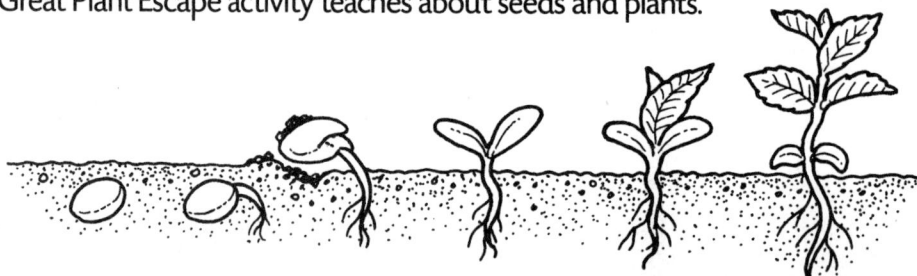

Mold

© 2001 Rigby

Key Words

mold, growing

Subjects

science, math

Get Ready

- Slices of bread
- Plastic sandwich bags
- Water to moisten some pieces of bread
- Hand-held magnifying glasses
- File folders, one for each child
- Preview the Internet site below for "Fun Facts About Fungi."

___

A

- Hold up a slice of bread. Ask: *What do you think can grow on this bread? Let's find out.*

- Moisten several slices of bread; leave several other slices dry. Let them sit in the open air for a few hours. Then remoisten the slices and place each slice—both moistened and dry—in a sealed plastic sandwich bag.

- Have children make a drawing of the slices of bread as they appear now on the left side of the file folder—both the moist and the dry slices. Have them label these with the date and time. Have children observe the slices of bread on a daily basis. Ask children to predict what, if anything, will happen. Say: *Show me what is alike/ different. Tell me what you see.*

- After several days, mold will grow first on the bread that was moistened. Ask children what it could be. Have them observe the mold with a hand-held magnifying glass and draw a picture of it on the right side of their file folder. Also note the date and time. Ask children to describe what they see. Tell them this is called *mold*. Mold is a living thing that grows. Help children to calculate the number of days it took the mold to grow.

Re-source

www.herb.lsa.umich.edu/kidpage/factindx.htm
"Fun Facts About Fungi" provides background information for the teacher.

Growing Things

Key Words

plant, seed, roots, leaves, stem

Subjects

science

Get Ready

- 16 pinto or lima beans, soaked overnight
- 2 paper cups and 2 glass jars
- Paper towels and blotting paper
- Preview and download pictures and activities from the Internet sites below.

- Show the children the diagram of a plant downloaded from the Internet site. Ask them what they recognize on the diagram.

- Tell children they are going to watch things grow in four different ways.

- Plant four beans each in the paper cups. Cover the beans with half an inch of soil. Place one cup in a sunny spot; the other in a dark place.

- Line the inside of two glass jars with blotting paper. Fill the center of each jar with crumpled paper towels. Saturate the blotting paper and paper towels with water. Pour off any remaining water. Push four beans about half an inch from the top. Keep out of direct sunlight until leaves have sprouted.

- Water the soil in each container just enough to dampen the soil. Check the containers everyday to make sure they are moist. Add water as needed.

- Watch for the beans to sprout after about one week. After the seedlings have grown an inch above the glass jar, set one of the jars on its side. After a few days, examine what has happened. Have the children pantomime and tell how the plants are growing in each container. When the plants have reached full growth, use the Internet diagram as a reference to identify different parts of the plant. Make a class drawing. Use the diagrams to label and talk about what parts of the plants grow up, which plant grew fastest, which one grew slowly. Help the children draw conclusions about how a plant grows well.

Re-source

http://tqjunior.thinkquest.org/3715/index.html.
Download and print out the diagram of the plant.

http://www.urbanext.uiuc.edu/gpe
The Great Plant Escape is an activity that teaches about seeds and plants.

Roots, Stems, and Leaves

Key Words

plant, roots, stem, leaves, above, below

Subjects

science, health

Get Ready

- Copies of Reproducible 24, one per child
- Sticky notes
- Download a diagram from the first Internet site below. Preview the second site to extend the activity.

B

- Distribute the picture cards on Reproducible 24. Cover the words *above* and *under* with sticky notes. Have children identify the vegetables. Ask: *Does it taste good/bad/soft/hard?*

- Tell children that sometimes we eat the part of plants growing *above* the ground, and sometimes we eat the part that grows *under* the ground. Have children accompany you with hand motions as you demonstrate *above the ground* and *under the ground*.

- Hold up each picture card and ask children to guess whether the vegetable grows above the ground or under the ground. Encourage discussion. Remove the sticky notes. Separate the vegetables into correct categories: *above* or *under* the ground. Have children name with you all the vegetables in each category.

Re-source

http://dallas.tamu.edu/weeds/anat.html
Download plant anatomy and the description of the structure and parts of a plant.

www.dole5aday.com
Provides a coloring book and information for children about fruits and vegetables.

under

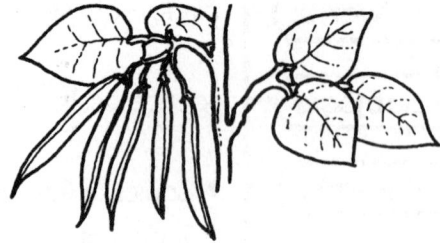

above

under

above

above

above

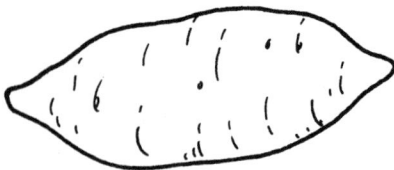

under

under

Growing Colors

Key Words

names of colors, names of fruits and vegetables

Subjects

science, health

Get Ready

- Gather assorted fruits and vegetables (real or plastic models) and place in a covered basket or container.
- Large squares of colored paper with colors corresponding to the fruits and vegetables
- Reproducible 25, one for each child, and set of word cards
- Scissors, paste
- Preview the Internet site below for a color chart.

B

- Give each child one or more pieces of colored paper. Have children identify the colors and name fruits, vegetables, and other things that are that color.

- Uncover the container of fruits and vegetables. Have children match the colors and name the fruits and vegetables. If you are using fresh fruit, cut open an apple and orange to show the seeds and identify the colors.

- Distribute Reproducible 25 with a set of word cards. Have children match the word to the picture. When all the word cards are correctly in place, have them paste and color the fruits. While the children work, cut up the fruits and raw vegetables and have some of the children help serve them as a snack. *Always check for food allergies before serving food to children.*

Re-source

http://www.englishclub.net/reference/vocabulary/col.htm
This site contains a color chart.

Match the word to the picture. Paste. Color the picture. ✂

| apple | orange | lemon | grapes | carrot | beans | corn | tomato |

The Egg

Key Words

egg, hatch, bird, chicken, reptile, snake, lizard, turtle

Subjects

science

Get Ready

🔖 Pictures of eggs from various animals and pictures of the adult animal. An excellent illustrated book is *Chickens Are Not the Only Ones* by Ruth Heller, Econo-Clad Books, 1999.
- Duck, goose, or bird egg
- Metal fasteners
- White construction paper or file folders
- Make egg shapes from sturdy cardboard to use for tracing, as many as necessary.
- Preview the Internet site below for background.

B
- Hold up an egg and ask: *What comes from this egg?* Accept reasonable guesses and list them on the board. Show egg pictures and ask the same question. Tell children these animals lay eggs: birds, reptiles, and turtles. Show pictures of the adult animals and have children identify them.

I
- Tell children they are going to make their own egg for whatever bird, reptile, or turtle they choose. Try to have books with pictures of eggs available so that children can see how big they should draw the egg.

B
- Have the children draw an egg shape on a file folder or construction paper. Children should cut out two egg shapes to be placed on top of each other and joined with a metal fastener. The top shape should be cut down the middle in zigzag fashion to represent a cracked egg. Overlap it slightly at the top and push the metal fastener through. The egg shape underneath is where children should draw their desired animal.

Re-source

http://www.edu.leeds.ac.uk/~edu/technology/epb97/forest/k_egg.htm
View a diagram of a bird egg.

The Life Cycle of a Butterfly

Key Words

life cycle, frog, egg, tadpole, butterfly, caterpillar, chrysalis

Subjects

science

Get Ready

- Analog clock
- Art supplies (scissors, glue markers crayons)
- Reproducible 26, one per child
- Preview the Internet site below for background and to extend the activity.

I

- Model, then ask volunteers to pantomime things that they do from the time they get up to the time they go to bed. Display the clock and set it to specific times that match a fairly standard schedule (example: 7:00 a.m., 12 noon, 6:00 p.m., 9:00 p.m.). Introduce the terms *first, next, last.* For example: *First I get up. Next, I brush my teeth. Then I put on my clothes. Last, I eat breakfast.*

- To explain how life occurs in cycles, draw a circular pattern of arrows on the board and ask: *What is the first thing you do in the morning? What do you do next?* and so on. Highlight the major events of the day between the arrows until you reach bedtime. Stress that this is a cycle that repeats each day.

I

- Tell children that there are cycles in the animal world, too. Using the cards from reproducible 26, take children through the life-cycle patterns of the frog and butterfly. Have them cut and glue the pictures on the circular pattern as you explain. They may also color the illustrations.

A

- Encourage volunteers to retell the life cycles of these two animals while in small groups. Emphasize *first, next, last.*

A

- Again as a whole group, ask children to compare and contrast the frog and butterfly life cycle. How are they different? How are they the same?

Re-source

http://www.mesc.usgs.gov/butterfly/butterfly-life-cycle.html
Children's Butterfly Site

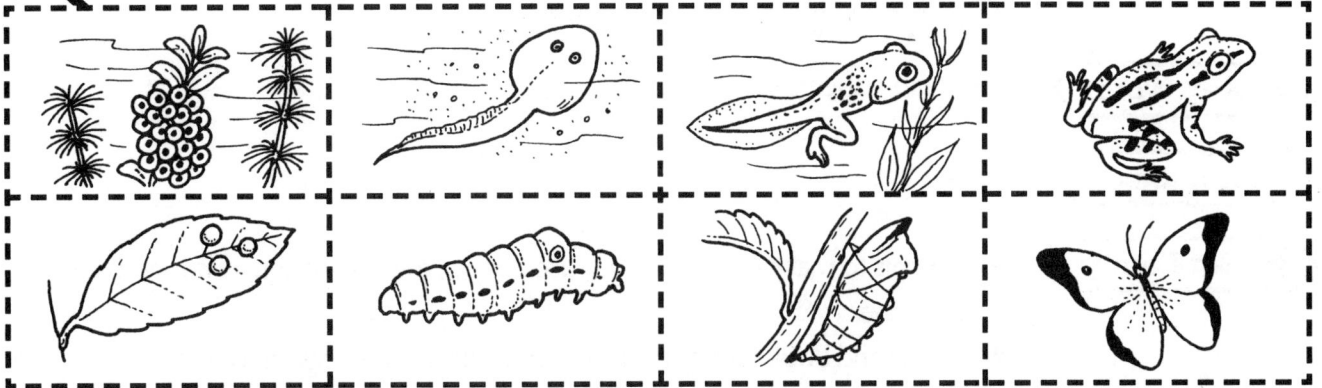

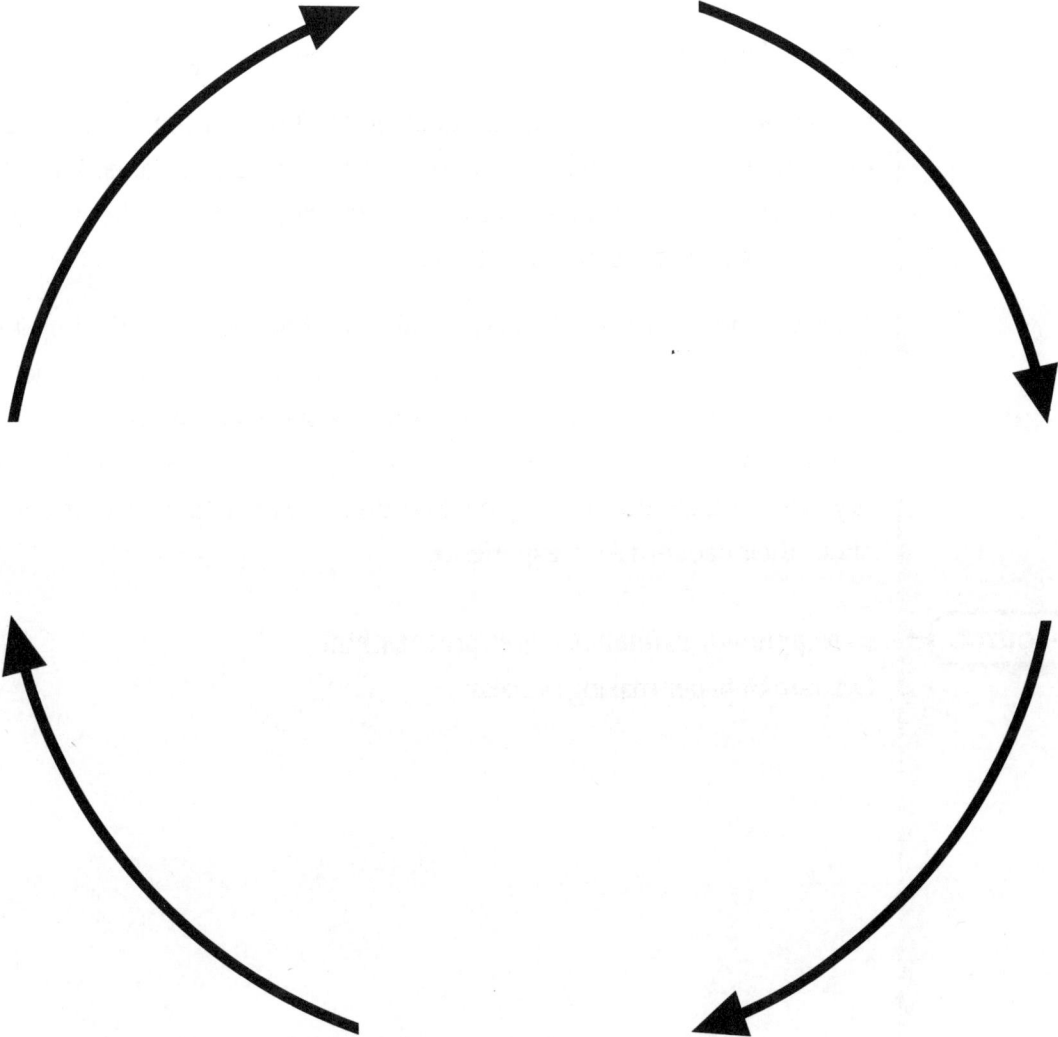

Growing Paper

Key Words

tree, pulp, paper, processing

Subjects

science, art

Get Ready

- Materials to make paper: blender, used paper, measuring cup, window screen, newspaper
- Preview and bookmark the Internet site below for a diagram of the paper-making process.

---

❶

- Hold up a piece of paper and ask children where it comes from. After allowing them to respond, explain that it is made from trees and that this is an ancient process. Tell them they will visit a Web site to see how paper is produced from trees.

- Connect to **www.ppic.org.uk/htdocs/paper/process.htm** to view a detailed diagram of the paper-making process from tree to pulp to paper. After children have discussed the vocabulary involved with this process, tell them they are going to make paper in class from used paper.

- Gather paper from school recycling bins and have everyone rip it up into very small pieces until you have about two cups. Place the pieces in a blender with 1 cup of water and blend until smooth. The mixture should be like mush. Pour this mixture onto a fine mesh screen while holding it over a sink. Spread it out and let it dry overnight. On the next day, have children use the paper to write and draw about their paper-making experience.

Re-source

www.ppic.org.uk/htdocs/paper/process.htm
Diagram of paper-making process

Growing Food

Key Words

apple, skin, pulp, stem, core, seeds

Subjects

language arts, health

Get Ready

- A variety of apples
- Knife for cutting apples
- Supplies for making applesauce and toppings
- Preview and download materials from the Internet sites below to extend the activity.

B • Display several different kinds and colors of apples. Pass them around so that students can see, smell, and touch them. Ask about the colors, shapes, and sizes. Ask: *Where do apples come from? Why are apples good to eat?*

I • Introduce vocabulary about the apple (*skin, pulp, stem, core, seeds*) as you cut open one apple lengthwise to view the inside. Then cut one apple across the width. Observe the star shape inside.

I • Ask: *Do all apples taste the same? Let's find out.* Have each child wash one apple and bring it to you to cut into slices. Pass around little pieces of the same apple and get a group consensus about how it tastes (sweet, tart, sour, bland). Tell them the name of each apple.

B • Make applesauce (raw or cooked) with the extra apples and serve with a choice of toppings such as cinnamon, raisins, nuts, bananas, chocolate chips, shredded coconut, and so on. *Always check for food allergies before serving food to children.*

Re-source

www.msc.cornell.edu/~weeds/SchoolPages/Appleseed/welcome.html
Learn about Johnny Appleseed (John Chapman)

www.bestapples.com
To ask questions about apples, download a coloring book, or view a slide show go to the Just for Kids section.

Growing Taller

Key Words

growing, taller, every day

Subjects

music, math

Get Ready

- Print the words of the "Growing Taller" song on large newsprint.
- Download a melody track for the song from the Internet site below.

B

- Introduce this song by using hand motions to indicate growing taller. Use fingers to indicate the number of inches. Sing one verse and have children repeat in a call and response fashion until familiar.

> **Growing Taller** (sung to the tune of "Frere Jacques")
>
> *Growing taller, growing taller*
> *Every day, every day.*
> *Now I'm one inch taller (and I'm growing taller)*
> *Now I'm two inches taller (I'm not growing shorter)*
> *And that's okay, that's okay. (Inch by inch, Hurray!)*

B

- Each time the verse is sung add more inches (Example: three and four, five and six, and so on) until ten inches are reached.

B

- Direct children to the song on newsprint. Invite volunteers to identify words in print.

I

- *Optional:* After children become very familiar with the song, explore ways that they could adapt the song by using different words. For example, change *taller* to *smaller* or *smarter* and change other words as needed. Encourage children to think about what makes sense.

Re-source

http://www.mwfp.com/fisher_price/sounds/pocket_radio66.au
Visit this site to hear a music-box rendition of the "Frere Jacques" melody.

Foods That Help Us Grow

Key Words

breakfast, lunch, dinner, the names of food, words for plants

Subjects

science, health

Get Ready

- Five sheets of chart paper
- Draw a clock face on the board.
- Preview and bookmark the Internet sites below.

1

- Help children understand that eating right is one way that helps them grow. Ask children to name things that they like to eat. List the foods. Say each word and have children tell at which meal they eat that food. Draw a clock face on the board and have volunteers draw the time for each meal: breakfast, lunch, and dinner.

- Tell children that they are going to keep a log of what they eat for lunch for a week. After lunch each day or in a following class, brainstorm everything they had to eat. Have them draw pictures on the chart paper. Help children label the pictures.

- Help students identify the foods and food groups on the food pyramid. Help children match the foods they ate for lunch to the correct food group on the food pyramid. Go to **http://schoolmenu.com/menus.htm**. Click on your state and find your school district to find out what's for lunch this week or see what students around the country are eating. Match the foods on the food pyramid to those on the lunch menu.

Re-source

http://schoolmenu.com/menus.htm
This site provides school menus from around the country.

http://www.usda.gov/cnpp/KidsPyra/index.htm
Select the poster-sized pyramid to download and print.

© 2001 Rigby

Critters and Creatures A-Z

Key Words

Alphabet letters A to Z, names of animals from A to Z

Subjects

science, language arts

Get Ready

- 26 sheets of chart paper or tag board, each sheet labeled with a different upper-case and lowercase letter of the alphabet
- Reproducible 27, one per child
- Art supplies (scissors, markers, and paste)
- Preview and bookmark the Internet sites below.

B

- Distribute Reproducible 27. Invite the children on a walk through Alphabet Jungle with three animal friends. Help children identify the three animals (alligator, bear, cat). Write the words on the board and have them sound them out, emphasizing the initial letter and sound. Ask them to look at the picture and find the letter that begins each animal's name.

I

- Have the children work individually or in pairs to find the letters. When they have finished, select individual letters. Brainstorm names of animals that start with that letter.

B

- Go to **www.infostuff.com/kids/a.htm**. Have the children go screen by screen as they identify the letter, read the animal's name, print it, and paste it on the correct alphabet page on the chart paper. Bind together into a big book. From time to time, feature a letter or letters. Go to **http://www.scz.org/animals**. Click on an animal to view fact sheets about the different species.

Re-source

www.infostuff.com/kids/a.htm
http://www.scz.org/animals

In Alphabet Jungle

Three friends go for a walk in Alphabet Jungle.
What letters do you see?

Animal Babies

Key Words

If you were born a _____ , kitten, seahorse, chick, porcupine, whale, opossum, snake, bear cub, deer mouse, elephant, tadpole, baby

Subjects

language arts, social studies, science

Get Ready

If You Were Born a Kitten by Marion Dane Bauer, illustrated by Joellen McAllister Stammen, Simon and Schuster, 1997.
- Sticky notes
- Mural paper and art supplies (markers, crayons)
- Preview the Internet site below for more fun with animals.

B

- As you preview the story, go picture by picture and have the children try to identify each animal. Encourage them to move and make sounds like that animal. When the animal has been correctly identified, write the name on a sticky note and place it on the page.

- Write this sentence frame on the board.

    If you were born a _____ , you'd _____ .

Read the first page, emphasizing the sentence *If you were born a kitten, you'd _____.*

Reread the story, encouraging the children to join in on the repetitive first line or pause so that the children can supply the name of the animal. Invite volunteers to act out parts of the text, adding animal-like movement and sound.

- Post the sticky notes randomly across the mural paper for reference. (Make duplicate labels, depending on class size.) Assign each child at least one animal. Tell children to imagine they are that animal. Have them draw and write about themselves doing things as that animal. Select children to be experts on particular animals. Have the "animal expert" replace the sticky note with his or her animal name and join you in rereading the appropriate page in the text. Encourage children to act out the animals as they read. Invite the class to join in playing together as each one of their animals.

Re-source

http://www.zooweb.net/
Search here for information about and pictures of animals. Also do a search under the name of your local zoo to find its Web site.

© 2001 Rigby

Animal Actions

Key Words

crawl, swim, jump, walk

Subjects

science, language arts

Get Ready

- Large poster board or newsprint, divided into 4 columns
- Index cards with key words
- Paper bag in which to place animal pictures from Internet sites
- Tape
- Writing paper
- Reproducible 28, one per child
- Download and printout pictures from the Internet sites below.

B

- Introduce the words *crawl, swim, jump,* and *walk* by showing the words one at a time on index cards and helping children to sound them out. Demonstrate each word and have children mimic your actions. Mix the cards up and show them again to provide additional practice. Stick the index cards on top of the 4 columns on the poster board.

B

- Tell children that both humans and animals do these actions. Invite a volunteer to pull one picture out of the "animal bag" and identify the animal, if possible. Choose whether that animal crawls, swims, jumps, or walks. Some animals can fit into more than one category so encourage discussion. Invite others to continue the process.

I

- After at least one animal has been identified in each column, hand out the reproducible picture cards and work together to identify the animals. Model as children write *crawl, swim, jump, walk* across the top of a sheet of paper. Then have children cut out the picture cards and sort them on their charts. Again there will be some animals that can fit into more than one category. Allow for personal choice and discussion.

Re-source

http://www.webclipart.about.com/internet/webclipart/msubmenu1.htm
This site provides links to animals, insets, marine life, and other clip art.

You can also search **http://www.yahooligans.com** for an additional source.

Animal Shapes

Key Words — shape words, tangrams, goose, rabbit, fox

Subjects — science, art

Get Ready
- Reproducible 29, one per child
- Construction paper
- Preview the Internet sites below for information about tangrams.

---

①

- Introduce children to the word *tangram* by showing them the reproducible and talking about the shapes they see. Tell them that a tangram is a Chinese puzzle from long ago. People put the shapes together in new ways to make objects and animals.

- Children should cut the shapes to make seven pieces. Have the class brainstorm the names of some animals they have been studying about in class. Make a list on the board.

- Challenge the class to use the shapes to make tangrams of animals. When a child puts together a tangram, he or she should also trace it so others can learn how to make it.

- Put together a class tangram book, using shapes cut from construction paper. Children can each be responsible for a page in the book. In addition to the tangram, they can dictate or write the name of the animal and two or three facts about it.

Re-source

There are a number of excellent, child-oriented Web sites dealing with tangrams.
http://www.geocities.com/tangramagicus
http://www.kidsdomain.com/down/mac/tangram.html

tree

goose

child

rabbit

fox

An Animal Song

Key Words

bear, mountains, see, over, around, under, through

Subjects

language arts, music, art

Get Ready

- Reproducible 30, one for each child and one for classroom use
- Two craft sticks for each child
- Art supplies (crayons, markers, glue, scissors)
- Preview the Internet site below for background.

B

- Tell children that they are going to learn a song about a bear who liked to walk and climb the mountains. Show your stick figure of the bear and mountain. Identify them.

- Sing "The Bear Went Over the Mountain" using your stick figure. Encourage children to join in as the verses repeat.

> The bear went <u>over</u> the mountain, the bear went <u>over</u> the mountain, the bear went <u>over</u> the mountain, to see what she could see.
> And all that she could see, And all that she could see
> Was the other side of the mountain, the other side of the mountain, the other side of the mountain, was all that she could see.
> So she climbed <u>over</u> another mountain, she climbed <u>over</u> another mountain, she climbed <u>over</u> another mountain to see what she could see.
> Repeat from: *And all that she could see, and all that she could see*

- After children learn the song, have them cut out and color the bear and mountain, then glue sticks on the back of each. Cut a hole in the mountain as indicated.

- Sing the song again while children use their props. Substitute and demonstrate other prepositions such as *around, under,* and *through* instead of *over.* Children follow along singing and moving their bears.

Re-source

http://www.yahooligans.com/
Search under subject <u>bears</u>.
Link to pictures of and information on bears. Search sites for additional information.

© 2001 Rigby

Cut out the mountain and bear shapes.

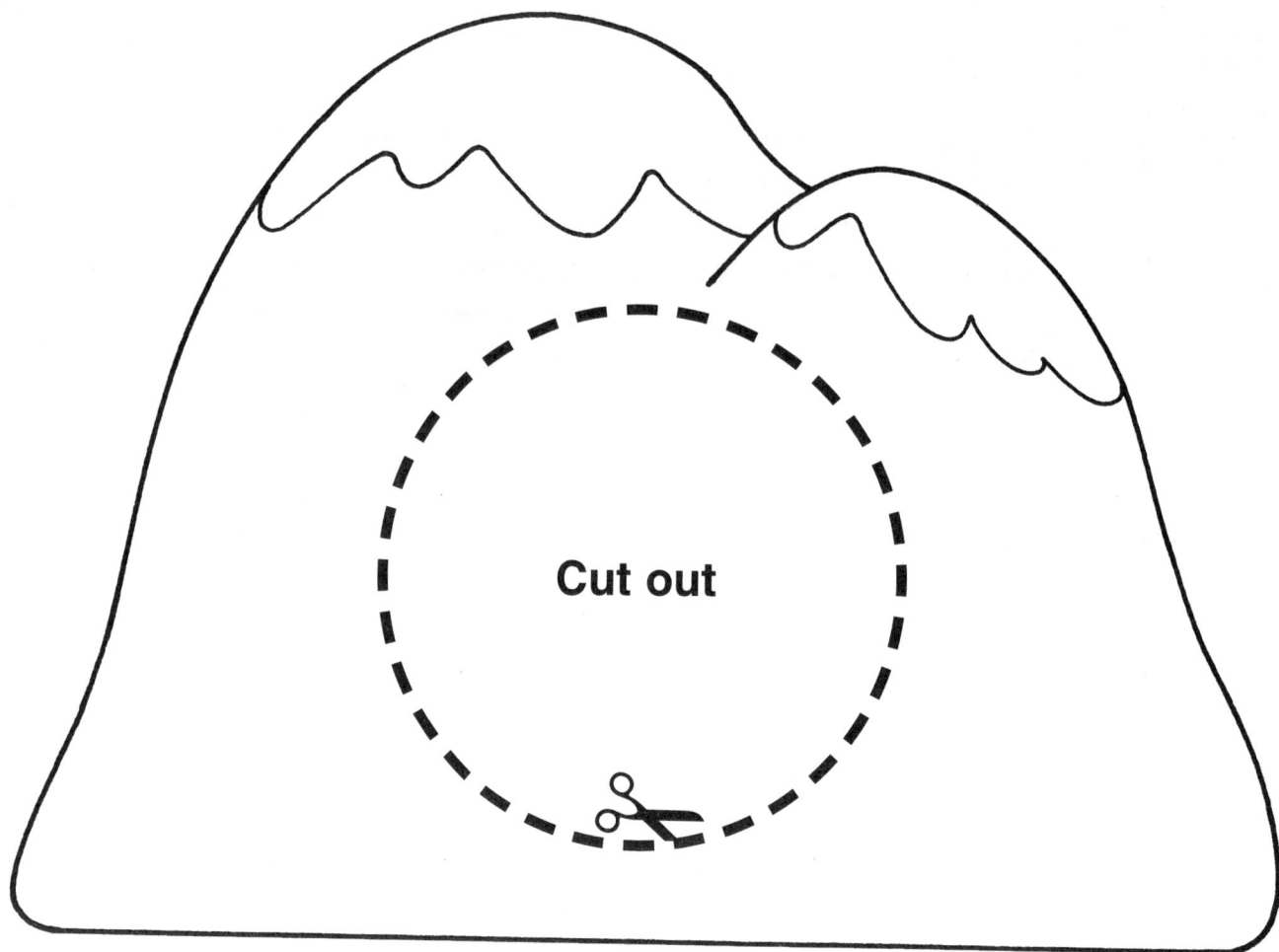

Cut out

Birds

Key Words

birds, names of birds, date, How many? What color? What size? What kind?

Subjects

science, math, language arts

Get Ready

● Prepare a chart with headers:
  Date   How many birds visited today?   What color?   What size?   What kind?
● Preview and bookmark the Internet sites below.

● Play the bird sounds from **birds.cornell.edu/BOW/index.html**. Tell the children to listen and ask them what they hear. Verify that they are listening to bird sounds. Go to the Internet site. Select different birds and listen to their sounds. Ask children to point to or name birds that they know. Invite the children to act out being birds. (Perhaps you might put on the goose sounds and have the whole class be a flock of geese.)

● Tell children they are going to become bird watchers. Work with the children to make a bird feeder. For instructions on making a simple one from a milk carton and on what to feed birds go to
http://www.dfw.state.or.us/ODFWhtml/Education/birdfeeder.html.
Hang the bird feeder outside the classroom. Familiarize children with the chart. On the first day, compile the information together. (Remind children to be quiet so they don't scare off the birds.) Then assign children to different days. You may wish to identify the birds from day to day.

● Compile the data and compare it from day to day. Ask questions, for example, *How many birds visited today? Three. One was brown. Two were blue.*

Re-source

www.dfw.state.or.us/ODFWhtml/Education/birdfeeder.html
Lists supplies to make a bird feeder and what kinds of food you will need.

birds.cornell.edu/BOW/index.html
This site provides bird sounds.

An Animal Fable

Key Words

lion, mouse, mice, sleeping, playing, mad, sad, hand, net

Subjects

language arts

Get Ready

- Flash cards for each of the key words
- Reproducible 31, one copy for each child
- Preview the Internet site below for a collection of Aesop's fables.

A

- Display the flashcard for *lion* and *mouse*. Have children say the word with you and then pantomime the actions of a lion or a mouse. Tell children they will meet a lion and a mouse in the story they are going to read.

- Distribute Reproducible 31. Read the story through once with the children. Encourage them to join in as they demonstrate familiarity with each rebus picture.

- Display each flashcard. Have children say the word with you and then match the flashcard to the picture on the reproducible. Read the story through again as children track the text and read along with you.

- Brainstorm animal names to replace *lion* and *mouse*; feeling words to replace *mad* and *sad*, actions to replace *sleeping, playing, eating*. Children can retell the story in groups with the new words.

- *Optional:* The Reproducible can be cut apart into sentence strips and shuffled. Then have children sequence the story *first, second, third;* or *first, next, last.* Advanced students may discuss the meaning of the moral of The Lion and the Mouse: One good turn deserves another.

Re-source

http://www.pacificnet.net/~johnr/aesop
A collection of Aesop's fables both with pictures and RealAudio narration as well as Aesop's fables lesson plans.

The Lion and the Mouse
An Aesop Fable

1 day a tired [lion] was [lion].

2 [mice] were [mice] nearby.

They awakened the [lion]. And he got [lion].

He grabbed 1 [mouse] in his [paw].

"Please let me go, Mr. [lion]," said little [mouse].

"You look so [mouse]," said the [lion].

So the [lion] let him go.

Another day little [mouse] went out to play.

He saw [lion] caught in a [net].

"Mr. [lion], 1 day you were nice to me," said the [mouse].

So little [mouse] [mouse].

And [lion] was set free.

Animals at the Zoo

Key Words

I'm going to the zoo to see some/a _____, words for zoo animals

Subjects

science

Get Ready

- Many Internet sites can supply or augment your animal picture library. Go to **http://www.zooweb.net/www.htm** and select a zoo. Select a variety of animal pictures and make labels. The animal pictures and labels may be prepared beforehand, or you might make your Internet search a classroom activity with a small group.
- Self-adhesive removable tape

B

- Invite children to go on an imaginary visit with you to the zoo. Before they go, ask them to brainstorm what animals they might see. Display those animal pictures from the Internet site. Invite the children to post the pictures somewhere in the classroom. Before they go to the zoo, work together and make labels for each animal.

- Walk around the classroom with the children, imagining you're spotting the different animals in the manner of "I spy." Encourage children to take on your role.

- Do an Internet search for animals at **http://www.zooweb.net/www.htm**. Make a name card for each animal and post the cards around the room.

- Use the pictures you displayed to play a game of "I'm going to the zoo." Start with the sentence frame:

      I'm going to the zoo to see some/a _____.

   Fill in the name of an animal. Then have a child repeat your sentence, choose another picture, and add that animal's name. Continue with different children, usually until you can list six to eight animals in a sequence and then start over.

Re-source

http://www.zooweb.net/www.htm
Click on a map to visit zoos all over the United States.

You may also do a search under the name of your local zoo
or visit the National Zoo at **http://www.si.edu/natzoo/**
or visit **http://dir.yahoo.com/science/biology/zoology/zoos/** for more pictures.

Celebrating New Classmates

Key Words

names of classmates, class, words of introduction

Subjects

social studies, physical education

Get Ready

- If this activity is done at the beginning of the school year when the children don't know each other's names, make name cards.
- Download the melody track from the Internet site below.

B

- Gather the children in a circle. Select one child to stand up. He or she walks around the circle as everyone sings.

> "Who's Who" (to the tune of "The Farmer in the Dell")
>
> [Child's Name ('s)] in our class.(repeat)
> Hi-ho, let's celebrate.
> [Child's Name ('s)] in our class.

The first child selects another child and they walk around the circle together while the class sings the new verse.

> [Child's Name] chooses [name]. (repeat)
> Hi-ho, let's celebrate.
> [Child's Name] chooses [name].

Continue until all the children and you are linked in a circle, holding hands.

- You may wish to remove nametags for this follow up. Review the alphabet and ABC order. Point to a child or call him or her by last name (Mr. or Ms. ____). Ask that child to come forward and start the line. In random order, ask another and then another. As each child joins the group, the children rearrange themselves to be in ABC order until all the children are lined up alphabetically.

- Have the children assume the role of teacher, selecting each child to come forward. Practice going in line as one introduces him or herself and the preceding child to the next child. For example, *Hi, I'm Rosa. This is Serge.*

Re-source

http://www.judyanddavid.com/
Hear "The Farmer in the Dell" by choosing the online songbook.

Celebrating People Who Care About Us

Key Words

I care about _____, words for special people

Subjects

social studies

Get Ready

- 3 sheets of chart paper, labeled *Home, School, Neighborhood*
- Pictures of people in action from newspapers, magazines, Internet sites
- Art and drawing supplies
- Download pictures from the Internet site below.

B

- Start with yourself, modeling the sentence frame:

    I care about _____ .

  After you give several examples, have the children respond. List their responses and suggest others as needed (the principal, police officers, firefighters).

- Talk about these special people, helping children understand that these are people at home, school, or from their neighborhood. Review the list and help the children categorize their responses and list them on the correct chart.

- Have groups of children make the chart papers into posters. They might use the pictures provided or photographs from home. Revisit the posters, adding to them as children recognize the growing number of people they care about. From time to time invite each of these people to class for a celebration day.

Re-source

http://stats.bls.gov/k12/html/edu_over.htm
Find pictures of people in different careers.

Celebrating Where We Came From

Key Words

map, north, south, east, west, oceans, continents, islands, names of countries

Subjects

social studies, geography, language arts

Get Ready

- In preparation for this activity, some children may need to ask their family members what country they came from.
- A world map
- Index cards, one for each student
- Preview and bookmark the Internet site below.

1

- Familiarize children with the world map. Point to the parts of the map that are *oceans, continents, islands*. Show directions: *north, south, east, west,* both in the context of the map and in the classroom. Invite volunteers to point to their countries of origin.

- Model dialogues. For example, *Where do you come from? I come from _____. My parents come from _____.* Continue until the children are comfortable enough to ask each other these questions. Select individuals to explore more about their countries on the Internet as their classmates observe. Go to **yahooligans.com.** Select Countries. Work with the children to find their home countries in the alphabetical listing. Help them select a Home Page or something of interest from their Country Index and print it out. (You will often need to read and shelter the English in the index.) Do the same for selecting and printing out the map of the country. Go to **http://www.atlapedia.com/**. Select Countries A to Z.

- Have each child write his or her name on an index card. For each child, display on the bulletin board an individual country map, the Internet printout, and the child's name written on the index card, connected to the map by a piece of yarn. Invite him or her to show and talk about the information displayed. You may wish to feature a different country or child each week. Invite children and school personnel who come from different countries to participate. Each Internet site is likely to provide you with such information as national flags, currency, tourist information, weather, museums, and zoo sites.

Re-source

http://www.yahooligans.com. Select Countries.

Celebrating In Cyberspace

Key Words

computer, screen, keyboard, mouse, disk, CD-ROM, printer

Subjects

language arts, math, technology

Get Ready

- Sticky notes
- A list of email addresses of people the children will know (for example: teachers, friends, family). Check your district's policy and always supervise children's correspondence on the Internet.
- Preview and bookmark the Internet sites below.

- Work hands-on with the children. Ask children to talk about what they already know about computers; what the computer can do; what parts of the computer they can name. Write the names of each part on sticky notes and label them (*screen, keyboard, mouse, disk, CD-ROM, printer*).

- Practice simple operations. Have children type in their names, addresses. Direct a child to print out the list. Go to **www.kidsdomain.com/clip/**. Select anything from the index, proceed screen-by-screen as they practice clicking, dragging and scrolling. Have each child choose a favorite icon from the list to click on, enlarge, and print.

- Go to the page you've selected on **www.bluemountain.com/index.html**. Choose a holiday, occasion, or subject you might like to celebrate. Have a volunteer select a card and print it. Familiarize children with addressing and filling it in. You may also have each print out a card and send it to another student by class mail instead of email.

Re-source

www.kidsdomain.com/clip/

www.bluemountain.com/index.html

Celebrating 100 Days

Key Words

100, one hundred, counting

Subjects

math, physical education

Get Ready

• Preview and bookmark the Internet sites below.

1

• Many schools around the world have special celebrations and activities for the 100th day of school. Discuss the number 100 with your students. What does it mean? What does it represent? Accept all responses. Tell the children that they will be celebrating the 100th day of school (usually the end of January or some time in February).

• Children can help to count on the calendar every day in anticipation. They can also help to make plans for the big event. On the 100th day, children can explore measuring time (for example, *What does 100 seconds of silence feel like?*), doing 10 kinds of exercises 10 times each, putting 100 pennies into a jar, tossing a coin for heads or tails 100 times and tallying the results, finding out where 100 steps will go, and so on.

Re-source

• Connect to **http://www.slec.kiz.in.us/~west/proj/100th/act.htm** to find suggested activities for the 100th day of school. You may also submit your favorite unique activity.

A Celebration Parade

Key Words

hard, soft, cold, warm, wet, dry, long, short, light, dark

Subjects

language arts, social studies, science

Get Ready

📖 ***What's What? A Guessing Game*** by Mary Serfozo, illustrated by Keido Narahashi, Simon and Schuster, 1999.

- Write a note telling parents about this class project, asking parents to allow their child to bring a toy or special thing from home. When possible, invite family members to come for the activity.
- Enlist volunteers–who may come from the upper grades–to bring in skateboards or wagons.
- Crepe paper, ribbons, colored paper to decorate the floats.
- Download march music from the Internet site below.

1

- Draw a big question mark on the chalkboard. Invite the children into a guessing game using the key words. (For example, *What's hard? What do you have that's soft? What do you see in the classroom that's long/short?*) Give examples. When the children are ready, have them ask simple questions of each other. Introduce children to the reading by telling them that they will play this guessing game as you read with them ***What's What?***

- Pre-teach any necessary vocabulary. Carefully preview the book so that you do not reveal the answers to the guessing game. You may wish to show only the pages with the questions *What's hard? What's soft?*, and so on. Use your preferred guided reading strategy to read the book. Depending on the language level of the children, stop after each question and invite guesses. Then proceed with the story.

- Tell children that they are going to celebrate this reading with a parade. Revisit the ending. Then brainstorm things that each child might have and cherish, like the puppy. Have the children make up what's-what riddles. Invite the children to decorate the skateboards or wagons as floats to carry their special things. Add instruments or put on marching music. Invite family and school friends as you celebrate with a parade of the children's everyday treasures.

Re-source

http://www.dws.org/sousa/ra/dws-ssf.ram
Play the Sousa march "The Stars and Stripes Forever."

Celebration Postcards

Key Words — landmark, proper nouns for the names of landmarks, postcard, address

Subjects — social studies, history, language arts

Get Ready
- Postcards to use as models
- 5 x 8 index cards, at least one per child
- Envelopes with cancelled stamps
- Art supplies (pencils, scissors, paste)
- Bookmark the Internet site below and choose landmarks.

I
- Invite children on an imaginary trip to see landmarks and places of interest. Go to **www.yahooligans.com/Around_the_World/U_S_States**. Select your state. Select the sites. As you show children the pictures, shelter the English and use TPR (Total Physical Response) to talk about the things you see. Ask questions and make statements, *Point to the _____. What do you see? I see the/a _____*. Have the children act out what they might do at each of these places.

A
- Pass around the model postcards. Check that children understand that a postcard is used to write about and share things that happen on a trip. Talk about things that they might say about some of the places that they visit online. Print out pictures or have each child select a picture to print out. Have children trim and paste down the pictures on one side of the index card. On the other side, have the children draw a line down the middle. Teach or review writing an address. On the right side, have them address the card. Use "My Friend" and the school address. On the left side have them write or draw about their imaginary trip. Finish by having them cut out cancelled stamps to put on their postcards.

A
- Place the postcards in a box or bag. Have each child select a postcard. Have the receiver and the sender show and talk about what they sent and what they received. Use the postcards as part of a bulletin board display perhaps named "Our Visit to _____."

Re-source
www.yahooligans.com/
You may do a search under National Landmarks.
http://www.thepostcard.com/
Visit this postcard store on the Web.

Celebration Music Makers

Key Words — dancer(s), musician(s), skip, jump, march, hop, shake, rattle, strum, direction words

Subjects — music, physical education, health

Get Ready
- Collect found and recycled materials to make music makers.
- For rattling: dried beans, small stones, paper clips
- For strumming: string, straws, rubber bands, wire
- For instruments: plastic containers, small boxes, paper bags, paper plates and cups, cardboard tubes
- Display rhythm instruments/pictures of instruments from around the world.
- CD/cassette player and appropriate music selections
- Download music from the Internet site below.

- Help children make instruments from the assembled materials. Use instruments and pictures that are displayed for models.

- Divide the class into dancers and musicians. Have the musicians begin to make sounds (*shake, rattle, strum*). Warm up the dancers with freestyle movement and then add commands (*dance, skip, jump,* and so on). Add direction words (*to the right, left, back, front,* and so on). Reverse roles and repeat often.

- Create a dance party. Encourage individuals or partners to invent their own dances. Use soundtracks available from the Internet sites or from world music sources, such as the tapes and CDs of Andean street musicians.

Re-source — **http://www.amazon.com**
Search music selections (folk songs, for example) and play sample tracks.

A Celebration Quilt

Key Words
celebration, quilt

Subjects
social studies, art

Get Ready

- Request families, friends, and faculty to lend you quilts. Display these around the classroom.
- $8\frac{1}{2}$ x 11 light-colored construction paper
- Art supplies (markers; scissors; scraps of colored cloth, ribbon, paper)
- Hole punch
- String, ribbon, or yarn for tying together the finished quilt
- Preview and download pictures from the Internet site below.

- Talk about the quilts on display. Help children understand that in addition to being blankets, quilts once were used to celebrate special events, such as weddings or births. Brainstorm and list what special days the children like to celebrate, encouraging them to name celebrations from their home countries.

- Demonstrate how to trace your hand. Partner children to help each other trace their hands on the construction paper. When they have finished tracing, guide children as you fill in each finger with words and/or pictures.

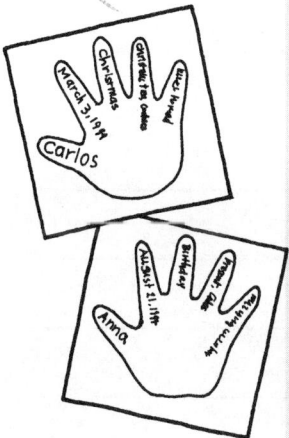

thumb	name
first finger	birthday
second finger	favorite celebration
third finger	celebration foods, toys, or decorations
fourth finger	something special about themselves (what they like to do or are good at)

Have children decorate their construction paper. Lay out the construction paper and punch two holes on the adjacent sides. Secure the sides with string, ribbon, or yarn.

- Select an individual each day to celebrate. Have that child point out and talk about his or her quilt square.

Re-source

http://americanhistory.si.edu/quilts/index.htm
This Smithsonian Institution site contains pictures of quilts and background and historical information on quilts.

MY INTERNET ADDRESS BOOK

Web address: _____

Comments: _____

_____

_____

Web address: _____

Comments: _____

_____

_____

Web address: _____

Comments: _____

_____

_____

Web address: _____

Comments: _____

_____

_____

Web address: _____

Comments: _____

_____

_____